Quilting
for the first time®

Quilting
for the first time®

Donna Kooler
Kooler Design Studio

Sterling Publishing Co., Inc.
New York
A Sterling/Chapelle Book

Chapelle, Ltd.

Owner: Jo Packham

Editor: Sharon Stasney

Staff: Areta Bingham, Kass Burchett,
Ray Cornia, Marilyn Goff,
Karla Haberstich, Holly Hollingsworth,
Susan Jorgensen, Emily Kirk,
Barbara Milburn, Karmen Quinney,
Caroll Shreeve, Cindy Stoeckl,
Kim Taylor, Sara Toliver,
Desirée Wybrow

 Kooler Design Studio

President: Donna Kooler
Executive Vice President: Linda Gillum
Vice President: Priscilla Timm
Editor in Chief: Judy Swager
Staff: Sara Angle, Lori Grant,
Karen Million, Sandy Orton,
Nancy Wong Spindler, JoLynn Taylor

Library of Congress Cataloging-in-Publication Data

Kooler, Donna.
Quilting for the first time / Donna Kooler.
  p. cm.
"A Sterling/Chapelle book."
includes index
ISBN 0-8069-8561-5
1. Patchwork. 2. Quilting. 3. Appliquâe. 1. Title.
TT835 .K664 2003
746.46--dc21

                                    2002015879

10 9 8 7 6 5 4 3 2

Published by Sterling Publishing Co., Inc.
387 Park Avenue South, New York, NY 10016
© 2003 by Donna Kooler
Distributed in Canada by Sterling Publishing
C/O Canadian Manda Group, One Atlantic Avenue, Suite 105
Toronto, Ontario, Canada M6K 3E7
Distributed in Great Britain by Chrysalis Books
64 Brewery Road, London N7 9NT, England
Distributed in Australia by Capricorn Link (Australia) Pty. Ltd.
P.O. Box 704, Windsor, NSW 2756, Australia
Printed in China
All Rights Reserved

Sterling ISBN 0-8069-8561-5

If you have any questions or comments, please contact:

Chapelle, Ltd., Inc.
P.O. Box 9252
Ogden, UT 84409
Phone: (801) 621-2777
FAX: (801) 621-2788
e-mail:
Chapelle@chapelleltd.com
web site:
www.chapelleltd.com

Table of Contents

Section 1:
Quilting Basics—10

Section 2:
Basic Techniques—28

Section 3:
Beyond the Basics—71

Quilting for the first time

Introduction

Quilting is an American art form that began in Colonial times. Every fabric scrap was precious to people, far from their former homes, who had to rely on supply ships for the most basic items. Keeping warm was a high priority, and luxuries were few and far between. But one thing our resourceful ancestors brought with them was a love of beauty. The American quilt combines frugality, utility, and beauty. The Baltimore Album Quilt Pillow (page 64) and the Traditional Nine-block Sampler Quilt (page 89) use designs that have been seen on the earliest quilts. Even though fabric today is plentiful, the art of quilting returns us to our Colonial roots.

Before the advent of the home sewing machine, quilts were made entirely by hand, and some people still enjoy doing all parts by hand. However, the majority of quilters today use sewing machines for the basic assembly sewing and save the handwork for the embellishment that will add the final touches.

The quilt has three basic elements—like a sandwich—with a top, filling, and bottom. These three layers are held in position with quilt stitches to prevent them from slipping during use. The edges are then bound.

The top can be simple and functional like the Quilted Envelope Purse (page 50), or elaborately patchworked like the Jewel-toned Eyeglass Case (page 76). Quilting, too, can be as minimal as the ties of the Tied Scrap Crib Quilt (page 30), or as elaborate as the central basket square of the Traditional Nine-block Sampler Quilt (page 89).

The filling, usually called batting, can be chosen for fiber content or "loft" (fluffiness). Fibers, such as cotton, that don't flame easily are a good choice for quilt projects like the House Pot Holder (page 46). Other quilt projects like the Christmas Tree Ornament (page 53) or the Comfort Tote Bag (page 35) need no batting at all.

The underside of the quilt is generally functional, to seal in the batting. It is usually chosen from a decorative fabric that coordinates with the quilt top. The raw edges are then held together with some sort of binding—again, functional, but also often decorative.

How to use this book

The projects in this book have been created to help you sample a wide variety of quilting techniques and designs in common use. Use it to discover some traditional favorites and as a starting point to develop your own creative expression.

This book assumes you have a basic knowledge of sewing and a sewing machine. Complete instructions and template patterns are included for making each of the quilts and other projects shown in this book.

We encourage you to carefully read the Quilting Basics on pages 10–27, study the diagrams and photographs, and read the individual project instructions before beginning a project. Don't feel tied to the examples, however. Additional quilting terms are included and defined in the Glossary on pages 110–111. Use the projects here to inspire you.

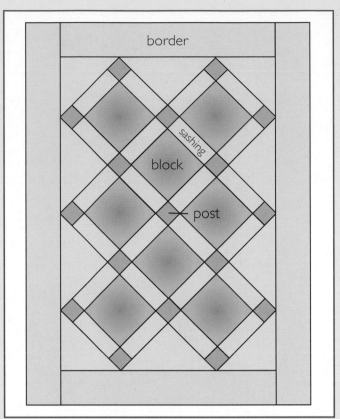

border

sashing

block

post

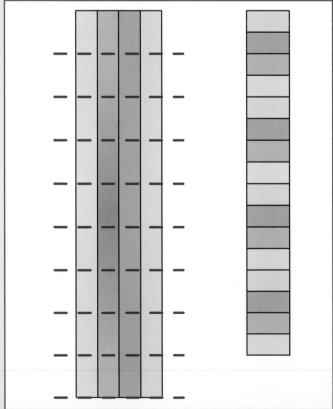

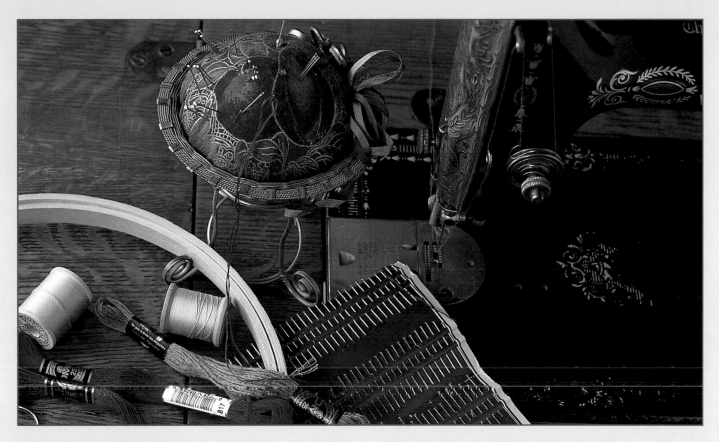

Section 1: Quilting Basics

What do I need to get started?

Unless otherwise specified, project items can be found in your local fabric or quilt shop.

For Body and Top of Quilt

Batting: polyester, cotton, or a polyester/cotton blend are recommended.

Fabrics: preferably 100% cotton decorative fabrics for the quilt top, quilt back, and binding.

Iron: one with both steam and dry settings.

Quilting hoop or frame: designed to securely hold the three layers of a quilt together while you quilt. A 14"–16" hoop is versatile and portable. Many different types and sizes are available at your local quilt shop, including a variety of large floor frames.

Quilting needles: short sturdy small-eyed needles for quilting patterns on the quilt.

Quilting pins: straight pins made especially for quilting. They are extra long with large round heads. Glass-head pins will stand up to occasional contact with a hot iron. Some quilters prefer extra-fine dressmaker's silk pins. If you are machine-quilting, you will need a large supply of 1"-long (size 01) rustproof safety pins for pin basting.

Quilting thread: stronger than general-purpose sewing thread. Some brands have a coating to make them slide more easily through all the quilt layers.

Sewing machine: a machine that produces a good, even straight stitch and has an adjustable zigzag. Be certain the tension is set correctly, and keep your machine oiled and serviced regularly. A walking foot, or even-feed foot, will help all three layers of the quilt move at the same rate over the feed dogs to provide a much smoother quilted project.

For Measuring, Marking, and Patterns

Eraser: soft white fabric eraser or white art eraser used to remove pencil marks from fabric. *Note: colored erasers may discolor the fabric.*

Freezer paper: heavy white paper, often used for template patterns. It has a plastic coating on one side that will adhere temporarily to fabric when pressed with a dry iron. (Look for this in your neighborhood grocery store.)

Marking chalk: light- or dark-colored chalk used to transfer patterns to fabrics. It rubs off easily.

Masking tape: 1"-wide masking tape used to secure the backing fabric to a flat surface when layering the quilt. Other widths can be used as a guide for straight or diagonal quilting stitches.

Permanent fine-point pen: used to mark templates and stencils and to sign and date quilts. Test pen on fabrics to make certain it will not bleed or wash out.

Quilt marking pencils: one of many available fabric-marking tools. A silver quilter's pencil is a good marker for both light and dark fabrics.

Quilter's ruler: a variety of sizes is available at most quilt and fabric supply stores. A standard 12" length is helpful.

Stencil/template materials: sheets of translucent plastic, often premarked with a grid. Made especially for making templates and quilting stencils. Some are iron-safe, others are not.

Tape measure: flexible 120"-long tape measure used for measuring a quilt top before adding borders.

For Cutting

Cutting mat: special mat designed for use with a rotary cutter. An 18" x 24" mat is a good size for most cutting steps.

Rotary cutter: round, sharp blade mounted on a handle with a retractable blade guard. This cutter is an essential tool for quick-method quilting techniques. It should be used only with a cutting mat and rotary-cutter ruler. Two sizes are generally available; we recommend the larger (45mm) size, which will cut through four layers.

Rotary-cutter ruler: thick, transparent acrylic ruler made specifically for use with a rotary cutter. It should have accurate $\frac{1}{8}$" crosswise and lengthwise markings and markings for 45° and 60° angles. A 6" x 24" ruler is a good size for most cutting. An additional 6" x 12" ruler or 12" square ruler is helpful when cutting wider pieces.

Scissors: sharp, high-quality fabric scissors. Use a separate pair of craft scissors for cutting papers and plastics. Smaller scissors are handy for clipping threads.

Seam ripper: useful for removing stitching.

For Sewing and Basting

Beeswax: used to cure and strengthen thread, particularly for making it easier to pull through multiple layers.

Embroidery flosses/needles: blunt tapestry needles designed to pull floss between the threads without piercing the thread fibers.

Embroidery hoops: two wooden hoops; one of which may or may not be clamped to a table. The free hoop is pressed down over the fabric to keep it taut for stitching.

Fray preventative: liquid sealant to keep raw edges from fraying while you are working.

Needles: two types of needles used for hand-sewing—betweens and sharps. Betweens are short strong needles used for stitching through layered fabrics and batting. Sharps are longer, thinner needles used for basting and other hand-sewing. For sewing machine needles, use sizes 10–14 or 70–90 universal (sharp-pointed) needles.

Thread conditioner: used to treat threads without leaving residue on fabrics.

Paper-backed fusible web: iron-on adhesive with paper backing, used to secure fabric cutouts to another fabric when appliquéing. If the cutouts will be stitched in place, use the lighter-weight web that will not stick to your sewing machine needle. Use the heavier-weight web for appliqués that are heat-fused in place without stitching.

Thimble: essential for hand-quilting. Available in metal, plastic, or leather, choose a size that fits comfortably.

Threads: several types for quilt making. General-purpose sewing thread is used for basting, piecing, and some appliquéing. Purchase high-quality cotton or cotton-covered polyester threads in light and dark neutrals, such as ecru and gray, for your basic supplies.

What do I need to know about fabrics?

This is one of the most fun and exciting parts of quilt making. In fact, the beautiful array of fabrics and colors often brings a new quilter to the hobby. Selecting fabrics isn't difficult—ask any quilter and you'll hear about the closet full of fabrics just waiting to be made into something glorious!

However, your beautiful quilt will be a piece of art—and you'll want to give a bit of thoughtful planning to your fabric selection. Fabric selection and layout is often a quilt's most creative aspect.

Choosing Fabrics

The first thing to consider is the fiber content; 100% cotton shrinks predictably and wears well and consistently. You can also use cotton blends, but be aware that washing can cause "pilling" as the different fibers react differently to wear. All the fabrics for a quilt should be of comparable weight and weave. However, if you've found a sheer or lace fabric you simply must include, baste the pieces onto an interfacing to make them comparable. If you are using a variety of different fiber blends, be certain to check for different rates of shrinkage and compensate accordingly.

Most domestic cotton and cotton-blend fabrics come in standard widths of 44"–45". Assuming that

approximately 1" of the selvage will be trimmed off, estimated yardage in this book is based on a final width of 42". Some imported or specialty fabrics come in widths of 28" or 36". Be certain to check the bolt-end of the fabric you've fallen in love with and adjust your yardage requirement, if necessary. When working with patterned fabrics, allow for design repeats.

Aside from design considerations, there are some things to consider when choosing prints. If you choose a directional print, you may need to add yardage if you want the print direction to go the same way. Most yardage widths are limited to 44"; so if your quilt is larger than that, the quilt back will need to be pieced. Choose a fabric that can be pieced without being obvious at the meeting points.

Using Prints and Color

Any examination of vintage quilts reveals that the use of color and prints has varied widely, following the fashions of the day. Compare quilts made in the 1930s to those made in the 1970s and you'll have no trouble telling them apart. There is no right or wrong in the prints and colors you choose, but there is a wide array of resources to help you. The library is full of books on antique quilts to contemplate. Your local fabric store or quilt shop is the best resource for books, magazines, inspiration, and other quilt enthusiasts to help you make print and color selections.

Choosing Battings

Batting is available in a variety of fibers, and choosing the right batting will make quilting easier. Bonded polyester batting is one of the most popular types. It is treated with a protective coating to stabilize the fibers and to prevent them from coming through the quilt fabric. All-cotton batting grips the quilt fabric and must be quilted more tightly than polyester. Cotton/polyester blends combine the best qualities of both polyester and cotton battings. Wool and silk battings are generally more expensive and usually must be dry cleaned. For fine hand-quilting, choose a low-loft batting in almost any of the above fibers. For machine-quilting, you will want a low-loft cotton or a cotton/polyester blend. If the quilt is to be tied, a high-loft batting, sometimes called extra-loft or fat batting, is a good choice. Whichever batting you choose, read the manufacturer's instructions closely for special information on care or preparation.

Preparing Fabrics

All fabrics should be washed, dried, and pressed before cutting. Press each fabric with a steam iron heat setting appropriate for the type of fabric you are using. Use spray starch to replace any lost crispness.

To check colorfastness before washing, cut a small piece of the fabric and place in a glass of hot water with a little detergent. Leave fabric in the water for a few minutes. Remove from water and blot fabric with white paper towels. If any color bleeds onto the towels, wash the fabric separately with warm water and detergent, then rinse until the water runs clear.

Tracing and Transferring Patterns

Most of the patterns in this book are full size for the projects created and can be traced directly from the book. If a pattern needs to be enlarged, take it to a photocopy shop and enlarge to the percentage indicated on the pattern instructions.

To trace a pattern for a template using acetate, follow the steps listed below.

1. Place the acetate over the pattern, then hold it in place.

2. Using a fine-point permanent marker, trace over lines of template. Use a quilter's ruler to keep the lines straight. Transfer all markings and dots to the template.

3. Use craft scissors to cut the template from the acetate.

To transfer a pattern onto freezer paper, follow the steps listed below.

1. Place the pattern and freezer paper on a light source, such as a window or a light-box.

2. Using a fine-point permanent marker, trace on paper side of the freezer paper over the lines of the pattern. You may need to make more than one of some of the patterns.

3. Use scissors to cut out the patterns from the freezer paper.

4. To get a mirror image, turn the pattern over and trace from the back side.

Cutting Fabrics

Fabrics have two grain lines: a straight grain, which runs along the length of the fabric (warp); and a cross grain, which runs along the width of the fabric (weft). The exact diagonal between these two is the true bias. Your choice of grain line will depend on how you want the fabric to react. Pieces cut on the straight grain will have the maximum strength and minimum amount of "give." Pieces cut on the cross grain will have moderate strength and stability. Pieces cut on the bias will have maximum flexibility and very little stability or strength. An easy way to

find the grain lines is to pull one thread from the width. Fabric on either side of the thread will pucker, allowing you to trim the raw edge precisely.

Strip-quilt cutting. Strip-quilting starts on the cutting board. In strip-quilting, a strip of fabric is cut to the length common to several pieces by the width of the fabric. (See Strip-quilting, page 19) Once you have a true cross grain, cut all strips from the selvage-to-selvage width of the fabric unless otherwise indicated. Trim off the selvages.

Rotary cutting. Rotary cutting has brought speed and accuracy to quilt making. Choose a rotary cutting tool that is comfortable to hold. Rotary cutters are extremely sharp, so be certain to read the product instructions carefully and observe the safety precautions. With a smooth downward motion, run the blade of the rotary cutter firmly along the right edge of the ruler. Always cut in a direction away from your body and develop a habit of closing the blade guard immediately after cutting.

What do I need to know about quilt tops?

Assembling the patchwork blocks is sometimes referred to as piecing. Quilters frequently use a modular approach, first piecing together the basic blocks, then setting them in simple rows or with sashing strips, posts, and outside borders. (See Glossary on pages 110–111) Precise cutting, followed by accurate piecing and careful pressing, ensures that all of the pieces of your quilt top fit together well.

Use a stitch length of 11 stitches per inch. Use a new sharp needle suited for medium-weight woven fabrics. Choose a matching or neutral-colored general-purpose sewing thread (rather than quilting thread). Never pull or stretch the fabric as you sew; even fabric cut on the strongest straight grain can be stretched somewhat. Because sewing can cause fabric layers to shift, pinning helps you achieve that coveted accuracy—especially for matching seams perfectly.

Basic Block

The first element generally constructed is the basic block. Simple shapes like squares and triangles can be cut from measurements, as in the Tied Scrap Crib Quilt (page 30). Strip-quilting is a quick way to cut multiple pieces of the same width.

You can use patterns for blocks like the Drunkard's Path Block (page 105), or templates for pieces to be appliquéd. Patterns in this book include a ¼" seam allowance. When a marking such as a dot or star has been given, transfer the marking to the cut fabric pieces. Some of the projects have included both patterns and templates. Templates in this book do not include seam allowances because they are used to cut a paper shape that will be appliquéd to the fabric before it is cut out. In these cases, you will have to add the ¼" seam allowance around the template on the fabric when you cut it out.

Setting Elements

Once the basic blocks are constructed, they are arranged in a "setting." The setting describes how the quilt is laid out and may include strips of fabric between blocks, called "sashing strips." Settings can also include squares of fabric between sashing strips that are called "posts." (See Figure SS1)

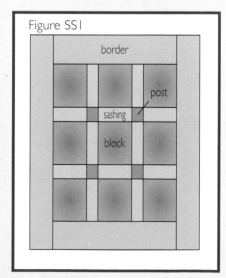

Figure SS1

border

post

sashing

block

A setting can be straight, as in Figure SS1 on page 17, or on the diagonal, as in Figure SS2. These

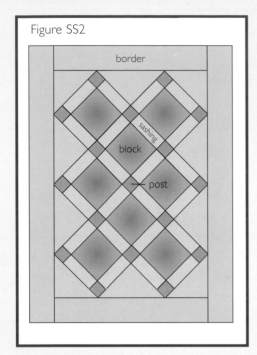

Figure SS2

border

sashing

block

post

diagonal settings require setting triangles to alternate triangular pieces that make the transition to the straight borders.

Borders can be used around the basic blocks as well as on the edges of the setting. Block borders can be very useful in evening out blocks that are slightly different in size. Check the size of each finished block before you begin to assemble the top. If there is a slight variation due to either fabric stretching or to inconsistent seam allowances, the addition of narrow borders around the block can compensate. The viewer will not notice that some blocks have a ½"

border and others ⅝" or ¾".

Borders cut along the straight grain will lie flatter than the borders that are cut along the cross grain. Squared borders are usually added first to top and bottom, then to the side edges. (See Figure SS3)

Borders that have mitered corners are often cut longer than the normal seam allowance to allow a working allowance. In mitered corners, (See Figure SS4) the strips are sewn just to the end of the seam allowance at the corners, folded and then pressed at a 45° angle, and sewn to the outer edge. (See Figure SS5) The working allowance is then trimmed off even with the raw edges of the sides to finish the corner.

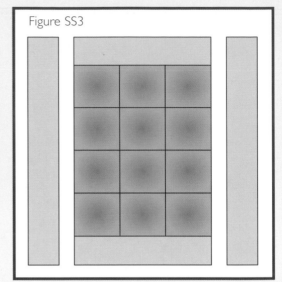

Figure SS3

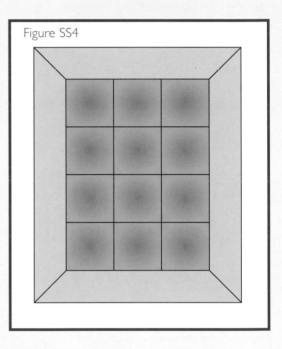

Figure SS4

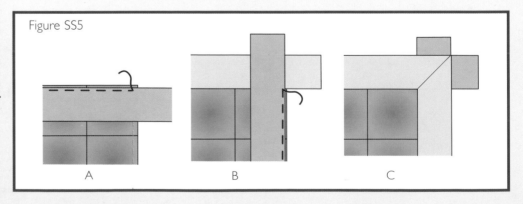

Figure SS5

A

B

C

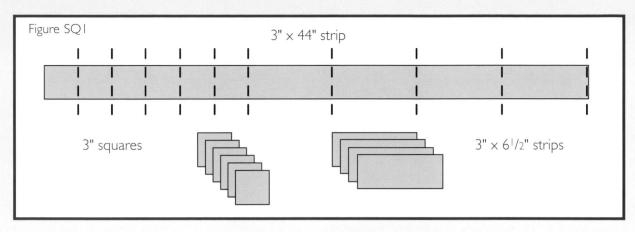

Figure SQ1

3" × 44" strip

3" squares

3" × 6½" strips

Strip-quilting

Strip-quilting is a popular construction method that saves time and can be used on blocks, settings, posts, or borders. The most basic use of strip-quilting is to simply cut a strip of fabric on the cross grain to the width that is common to the pieces you need. For example, a 3" strip 44" wide can be cut into six 3" squares and four 3" × 6½" strips. (See Figure SQ1)

In another method of strip-quilting, fabric strips are sewn together and then cut apart to make new shapes. (See Figure SQ2) Seminole patchwork is an example of how this kind of strip-piecing can create a dramatic effect. An example of how it can be used in a border is the Redwork Wall Hanging on page 84.

Strip-quilting is also done as a "stitch and trim" method, as in the Log Cabin Pincushion on page 61. In this method, the entire end of the cut strip is sewn to the starting piece, then trimmed to fit. The strip is then repositioned and the stitch-and-trim repeated.

Foundation Piecing

Working with small pieces can be challenging just because of their size. Foundation piecing and paper piecing are modern innovations that can be very useful when working on small pieces. In both cases, you rough-cut the fabric pieces, then trim them after sewing as you go. For this type of work,

a pressing and cutting area next to your sewing machine is very useful. Lower the ironing board to sewing level and use one end for cutting and the other for pressing. A small lamp nearby helps you view placement of the fabric through the foundation fabric or paper.

Foundation piecing is a way to stabilize the working area by sewing the small pieces directly onto a foundation fabric on which the pattern lines have been drawn. The fabric pieces can be rough-cut; they need not be exact because you will be sewing on the drawn seam line. Fabric pieces are placed on the back side of the foundation

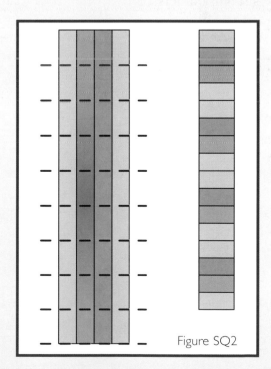

Figure SQ2

19

(without drawn lines); sewing is done on the front side of the foundation (with drawn lines). The pieces are positioned below the pattern shape, checked for position, then sewn, with right sides together, in the order given in the instructions. Each piece is folded and pressed before the next is added. The foundation fabric becomes part of the finished work. To sample this technique, try out the Christmas Tree Ornament on page 53.

Paper Piecing

Paper piecing is a foundation method that gives you perfectly consistent corners. It works in a similar way to foundation piecing, except you are working on paper rather than fabric. A paper pattern of the finished shape is created and fabric pieces are cut larger than the shapes (to add seam allowances). The pieces need not be exact because you will be sewing on the paper seam line. The pieces are positioned below the pattern shape (on the unmarked side of the paper), checked for position, then sewn with right sides together in the order given in the instructions on the right side of the pattern. Each piece is folded, trimmed, and pressed before the next is added. When all the pieces have been sewn together, the paper is removed.

Machine-appliquéing

Using the zigzag stitch on your sewing machine can be fun and an easy way to appliqué motifs to your quilt; however, getting the stitches even can take some practice. You may want to cut some trial pieces that have points and curves (both inside and outside) to practice. Simple shapes like stars and hearts can be a fun and challenging way to perfect your technique. Trying out shapes can germinate into ideas for entire quilts.

Cut your appliqué motifs from templates that don't include a seam allowance. Choose a stitch width that is in proportion to the size of the motifs

you are adding. A slightly open stitch length will help make your stitches look more consistent on curves.

When you need to change direction, whether on a curve, a corner, or a point, you will need to stop sewing with your needle down in the fabric, lift the presser foot and pivot the fabric to the new direction. Whether your needle is in a left- or right-swing position when you stop must be taken into consideration before you make the change.

On curves, the pivot can be slight, but to achieve an even transition, pivot at consistent intervals—every few stitches, if necessary. For an outside curve, pivot when the needle is in the right-swing position. For an inside curve, pivot when the needle is in the left-swing position. (See Figure MA1)

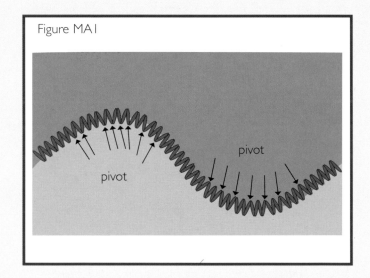

Figure MA1

When you come to a corner, you can either overlap the stitches or butt them to the next row. To overlap on an outside corner, stop the needle off the motif in the right-swing position. Lift the presser foot and pivot; lower the foot, turn the flywheel manually to position the next stitch to the left in the motif, and continue in the new direction. (See Figure MA2a on page 21) To butt the stitches on an outside corner, stop with the needle off the motif in

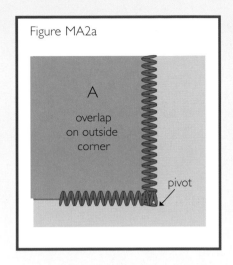

Figure MA2a

A

overlap
on outside
corner

pivot

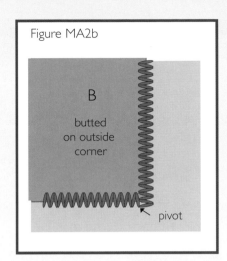

Figure MB2b

B

butted
on outside
corner

pivot

Hand-appliquéing

Hand-appliqué is often done very simply, using the needle to turn under the seam allowance as you stitch it to the base fabric with a blind stitch. This "needle-turn" method is easy to learn, but takes practice to build consistency.

A newer method using freezer-paper templates gives a consistent and accurate shape to the motif before you sew it to the quilt. Freezer paper has a plastic coating on one side that temporarily sticks to fabric when you iron it on, and pulls off easily when you have finished. You simply cut the freezer paper to the finished size of the motif and iron it to the wrong side of your design fabric. Cut out the motif ¼" larger all around than the freezer-paper template. With the freezer paper still adhered, you can press the seam allowance exactly over the edges of the freezer paper and baste it in position for a perfect finished edge. The parts of the motif that will be covered by another piece are not turned under or stitched.

the left position. Lift, pivot, and turn flywheel manually to position the next stitch to the right in the same hole. (See Figure MA2b) Inside corners are done in a similar way, but you need to stop and pivot before you reach the corner when you are the distance of your stitch width from it.

Outside and inside points are similar to corners, but the angles are narrower. You may want to use a narrower stitch width overall, or you can taper the stitch width as you approach the corner, ending with a width of 0 at the point, then increasing width as you change direction. (See Figure MA3)

Pressing Seams

In general, seams in quilting are pressed together to one side to create a stronger seam. On a patchwork quilt, the seams can go in any direction—up, down, left, or right—but this should be consistent throughout the quilt. When sewing a darker to a lighter piece, press the seams toward the darker fabric. On borders, seams should be pressed consistently as well, either toward the center or toward the outside.

Always press as you sew, taking care to prevent small folds along seam lines. When using exotic fibers, metallic embroidery, or beads, check iron setting carefully and use a pressing cloth to avoid damaging the materials.

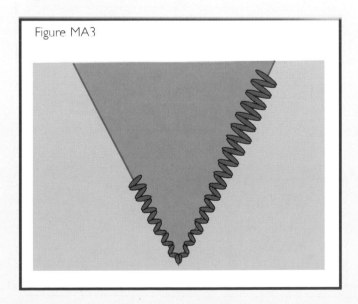

Figure MA3

Seam Allowances

For good results, it is also essential that you stitch with an accurate seam allowance. Incorrect seam allowances on your patchwork piecing will cause your finished measurements to be incorrect. Just $\frac{1}{16}$" too much on only eight seams will make the finished piece $\frac{1}{2}$" larger than the instructions have calculated. (See Figure SA1) This can make

Figure SA1

seam too small   accurate seam   seam too large

borders fit inaccurately, especially if you also have a fabric that gives or stretches. Unless instructed otherwise, place pieces with right sides together and match seam allowances—not necessarily the raw edges.

In quilting, seam allowances are generally $\frac{1}{4}$" unless otherwise indicated. Patterns in this book show the $\frac{1}{4}$" seam allowance as a broken line; however, when cutting squares from given measurements, check the gauge next to the presser foot on your sewing machine frequently to be certain you are accurate. This accuracy is the simple secret that the experts use to create beautifully crafted works of art. When joining small pieces, match the markings on the seam allowances, not the raw edges, to assure an accurate fit.

Templates (as opposed to patterns) generally don't include seam allowances. Templates are preferred when there will be no seam, such as in machine-appliqué, where the raw edge will be enclosed with a zigzag or buttonhole stitch. Templates can be purchased or made from patterns. If you are using a purchased template and want to use it as a pattern, you will need to add your own $\frac{1}{4}$" seam allowance.

Trimming Seams

The additional layers of fabric created by stitching two or more layers together have an impact on the final look of your quilt. They can detract from it by causing unsightly shadows and bulges, or they could create fullness where needed in places like bindings. As a general rule, trim patchwork seams to an even width, usually $\frac{1}{4}$", before layering and quilting the top. However, it is at times necessary to layer the seams to create a flat look, trimming one seam to $\frac{1}{8}$" and the second seam to $\frac{1}{4}$". (See Figure TS1)

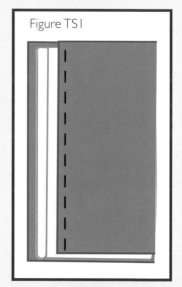

Figure TS1

If working with an irregular shape, you may need to slash or notch a seam allowance in order to reduce bulk or eliminate any folds.

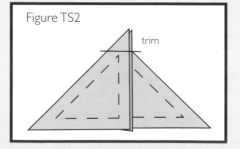

Figure TS2

trim

1

Points are often trimmed off very close to the seam line, as shown in Figure TS2.

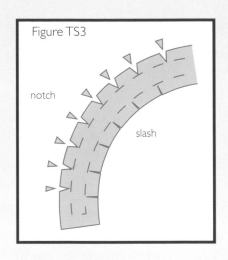

Figure TS3

notch

slash

*S*lash the inside curves to let them "give", *notch* the outside curves for "ease". (See Figure TS3) Use whichever stitch is appropriate for the situation.

How do I assemble a quilt?

Most quilts are comprised of three layers, like a "sandwich," a top design (often patchwork), the inner batting, and the bottom, or backing, fabric. The three layers are generally hand- or machine-stitched together in a decorative pattern, and the edges are then enclosed in a binding.

Preparing the Patchwork Top

Press the top and trim raw edges evenly. Square up the top if it has pulled out of shape while working. If you have an intricate quilting pattern, transfer it to the quilt top before assembling. Refer to Marking Quilting Lines on page 24. Straight stitching, outline stitching, and other simple quilt designs can be marked after assembly, as you quilt. On the back side of the quilt, trim any seam allowances and threads that may show through to the front of the quilt.

Preparing the Backing

To allow for slight shifting of the quilt top during quilting, the backing should be slightly larger on all sides than the top. Because quilts are often larger than standard fabric widths, quilt backings are very often pieced from one or more fabrics. Cut off the selvages before piecing the backing; you'll find they are more difficult to quilt through.

Layering and Basting the "Sandwich"

Place backing fabric on a clean flat surface, right side down. Use masking tape to secure edges of backing to work surface. Place batting on top of backing fabric. Smooth batting gently, being careful not to stretch or tear. Center quilt top right side up on batting.

Begin in the center of the top and work outward, smoothing fullness or wrinkles toward outer edges. Using glass-head pins, pin layers approximately every 8" along the top side of the quilt. If you intend to do hand-quilting, begin in the center of the top and baste the layers together with diagonal basting stitches in lines 4"–6" apart. (See Figure LB1)

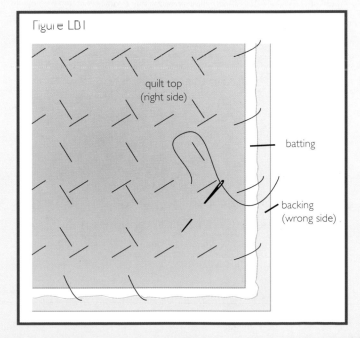

Figure LB1

quilt top (right side)

batting

backing (wrong side)

If you intend to do machine-quilting, use 1" rustproof safety pins to "pin-baste" all layers together, spacing pins approximately 4" apart.

How do I quilt the layers together?

Quilting Patterns

The stitching pattern you choose to stitch the sandwiched layers together has a great effect on the way your final quilt will look. These stitch patterns can be done by hand or by machine. Machine-quilting is sturdy and durable. Hand-quilting brings a delicate look. Whichever method you use, always baste the layers together first.

Marking Quilting Lines

Fabric-marking pencils, various types of chalk markers, and fabric-marking pens with inks that disappear with exposure to air or water, are readily available and work well for different applications. Lead pencils work well on light-colored fabric, but marks may be difficult to remove. White pencils are good for dark-colored fabric, and silver pencils show up well on many colors. Since chalk rubs off easily, it's a good choice if you are marking as you quilt. Fabric-marking pens make more durable and visible markings, but the marks should be carefully removed, following manufacturer's instructions. Press down only as hard as necessary to make a visible line.

When you choose to mark your quilt, whether before or after the layers are basted together, is also a factor in choosing a marking tool. If you mark with chalk or a chalk pencil, handling the quilt during basting may rub off the markings. Intricate or ornamental designs may not be practical to mark as you quilt; mark these designs before basting, using a more durable marker. Test your chosen marking tool on your fabric before using.

Quilting by Hand

The quilt stitch is a basic running stitch that forms a broken line on the quilt top and backing. Short, evenly spaced quilt stitches add dimension to your quilt. When you begin, concentrate on making regular, even stitches that follow the marked quilt design closely, with your needle entering and exiting in the center of the marked line. Space your stitches evenly apart, with the length of the stitch the same as the length of the space between them. Practice making your stitches as regular on the front as they are on the back. Good-quality quilting is seven-to-nine stitches per inch; experts sometimes achieve twelve or more.

To hide your knots, you can use what's called a quilter's knot. (See Figure QH1) When beginning a new line of quilting, knot the end of the thread. Insert the needle into the batting at a seam line on the quilt top, approximately ½" from where you wish to begin quilting. Bring the needle to the top where you wish to begin, and gently tug the thread to "pop" the knot through the top layer to "bury" it in the batting.

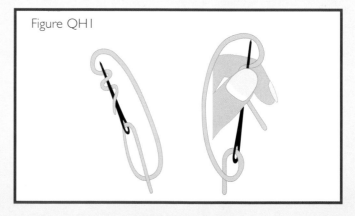
Figure QH1

At the end of a line of quilting, make a small backstitch through the top layer only. Pull the needle and thread to the top side. Wrap the thread around the needle twice, and holding the wraps with your free hand, pull the needle through. Tighten knot; then pull needle through, holding thread until it must be released. This creates a small

French knot close to the surface of the quilt. (See Figure QH2) At the point where the thread emerges, insert the needle into the batting and gently tug to pull, or bury, the knot below the surface. Bring needle out approximately ½" away and cut the thread.

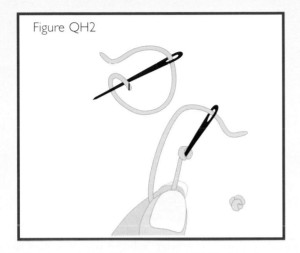

Figure QH2

Outline Quilting

This is a good choice if you want to add texture and complexity to a simpler patchwork. It is also commonly used around appliqué shapes. Quilt ⅛" to ¼" away from the patchwork seam allowances. Avoid stitching through seam allowances.

Quilting by Machine

Straight or curved lines can be marked on the fabric and stitched directly, using a special walking foot to help keep all the layers moving at the same speed. Many sewing machines also have special attachments that aid in machine-quilting.

Meander, or stipple, quilting is a series of close quilt stitches, using a meandering line. It is worked randomly by feel. When quilting in this manner, thread the needle of your machine with transparent monofilament thread. This will help your quilting blend in with your quilt-top fabrics. Use decorative thread when you want the quilting lines to stand out more. Use a darning foot, drop or cover the feed dogs, and set stitch length at zero. To secure the thread ends, pull up bobbin thread and tie both thread ends together. Bury the knot in the batting and cut threads near quilt surface.

Place hands lightly on quilt on either side of darning foot and begin stitching in a meandering pattern, guiding the quilt with your hands. The object is to make stitches of similar length and to not sew over previous stitching lines. Fill in one open area of the quilt before moving on to the next. (See Figure QM1)

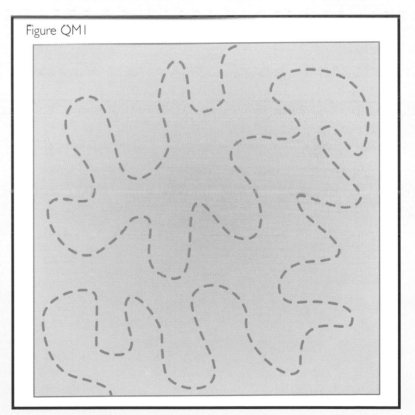

Figure QM1

Common Quilting Stitches

Baste Stitch. The baste stitch is 1"–2" long and worked loosely, 3"–4" apart. Basting is often done from the center outward, 4"–6" apart, in all horizontal and all vertical rows. Generally, knots are tied on top of the quilt for easy removal later on. (See Figure QS1)

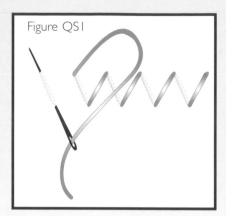

Figure QS1

Quilt Stitch. The quilt stitch consists of a series of straight stitches in which the stitch length is equal to the space between stitches.

As a quilting stitch, it is worked by holding the needle with your sewing hand and placing your other hand (with a thimble) underneath the quilt; use another thimble to push only the tip of the needle down through all layers. As soon as the needle can touch your thimble underneath, use that thimble edge to push the tip of the needle back up through the layers to top of quilt. The amount of the needle showing above the fabric determines the length of the quilting stitch. Rock the needle up and down, taking 3–6 stitches before bringing the needle and the thread completely through all the layers. (See Figure QS2)

Figure QS2

Straight Stitch. This simple stitch can be decorative or functional; the length, direction, and number of stitches can vary. Often used to connect repeating

patterns that don't meet evenly. (See Figure QS3)

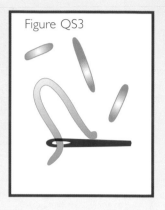

Figure QS3

Blind Stitch. This versatile stitch is worked inside the fold of a seam allowance and is used whenever you don't want stitching to show. It is commonly used to finish bindings and to sew appliqué motifs invisibly. The length of the stitches can vary. Begin with the starting knot on the inside of the seam allowance. With the tip of the needle, pick up just a few threads directly below where the seam edge will lie, then slide the needle back into the seam allowance. Bring it out again a short distance farther along the seam line and catch a few more threads. The length of the stitch interval can vary. The seams can be pressed beforehand, as in paper piecing, or you can use the needle to turn under the seam line as you proceed. (See Figure QS4)

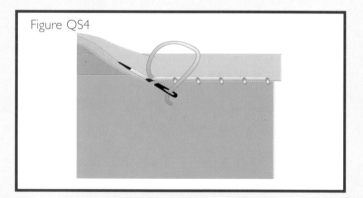

Figure QS4

How do I bind a quilt?

Bindings enclose the raw edges of your quilt. It can be decorative or inconspicuous, as small as ⅜" wide or well over an inch. It can be just one layer of fabric in thickness, or doubled to add strength. For stability on straight edges, bindings cut on the straight (lengthwise) grain or cross grain of the fabric are the best choice. Because of its stretchy quality, bias bindings work well for binding projects with curves or rounded corners. To piece or make continuous binding strips for either straight grain or bias bindings, sew strip ends, right sides together, on a 45° angle. Press seam allowances OPEN flat, and trim seam allowance. (See Figure B1)

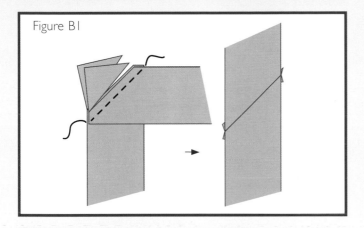

Figure B1

Mitered-corner Bindings

Mitered corners on bindings are similar to mitered corners for borders, except that the mitering must be done on both sides of the binding—the front of the binding that is attached by machine, and the back that is turned over and hand-stitched. They can be done with a continuous strip of binding fabric or with individual strips cut to size.

To prepare your quilt for binding, smooth out the quilt, top side up, on a clean flat surface. If you are basting by hand, pin the raw edges together approximately every 4"–6". Baste around the edge of the quilt just outside of the seam line with straight stitches, approximately 1" long and 1" apart. If you are basting by machine, you may wish to place your pins closer together—every 1"–2". Set the stitch length to a long baste stitch and baste as by hand, being careful that the layers don't shift. An even-feed foot on your sewing machine will help keep the layers from shifting. Before binding, trim off the raw edges of batting and backing. A rotary cutter works well for this. Trim off any loose threads at this time for a nice clean edge.

Wall Display

To display your quilt on a wall, attach a sleeve to the quilt back before the binding is added. Cut a piece of fabric 7" wide by the width of the quilt at the top minus 1". Press short edges under ¼" and ¼" again, then machine-stitch in place. With wrong sides together, fold piece in half lengthwise to form a tubular sleeve.

Sew binding, with right sides together, to quilt top, including backing and batting. However, before blind-stitching binding to back, pin the raw edges of the folded sleeve to the top raw edges of the quilt back. Stitch sleeve to top edge of the quilt back, then complete the blind-stitching, enclosing the raw edges of the sleeve. Blind-stitch the bottom of the sleeve to the backing, taking care not to stitch through to the front of the quilt. Insert a dowel through the sleeve.

How do I care for a quilt?

You'll want to be certain that your quilt stays in good condition. Keep it clean and air it regularly so dust and soil don't work into the fibers. Wash your quilt only when necessary, and then with a mild soap. Dry cleaning is not recommended because it leaves a chemical residue. Avoid displaying it in direct sunlight. Even indirect light through windows can fade colors over time.

Store your quilt in a dry place with a consistent room temperature. Avoid storing quilts in plastic; it traps moisture and encourages mildew. If you have the space, roll the quilt around a tube covered in cotton fabric. Folding is a potential danger to stored quilts, so layering crumpled acid-free tissue inside the folds helps support the fibers and protect them from long-term hazards. Fold it differently each time you refold the quilt. Enjoy it for years to come.

Section 2: Basic Techniques

1
technique

What you need to get started

Fabrics
44"–45"-wide 100% cotton

✂ ½ yard for binding

✂ 1⅓ yards for backing

✂ 1¾ yards scrap fabrics for patchwork top

✂ 45" x 60" high-loft batting

Additional items

☑ Hand-sewing needle

☑ Iron

☑ Large-eyed hand-sewing needle

☑ Quilter's ruler

☑ Rotary cutter and mat

☑ Safety pins

☑ Scissors

☑ Sewing machine

☑ Sewing thread

☑ Straight pins

☑ White mercerized thread

How do I construct a simple, tied, scrap quilt?

"Waste not, want not." To our grandmothers, this was simply common sense, and scrap quilts were probably some of the first quilts they ever made. The Tied Scrap Crib Quilt will allow you to put your favorite fabric scraps to good use.

Here's how:

Make the patchwork top

1. Choose fabrics that match the purpose and design of the quilt.

2. Cut a total of 288 3" squares from scrap fabrics.

3. Select two squares of one fabric and two of another fabric. With right sides together, sew one square of each different fabric together, taking ¼" seam allowance. Press seams to one side. Repeat. (See Photo A)

Photo A

Tied Scrap Crib Quilt finished size: 40" x 45"

4. Rotate a two-square unit and stitch to the other two-square unit to create a four-patch block. (See Figure 1) Use straight pins to help match center seam allowances as you sew. Make a total of 72 four-patch blocks.

5. With right sides together and matching seam allowances, sew a row of eight four-patch

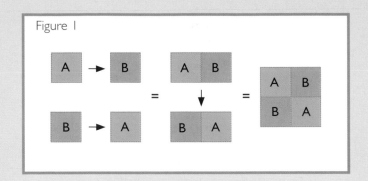

Figure 1

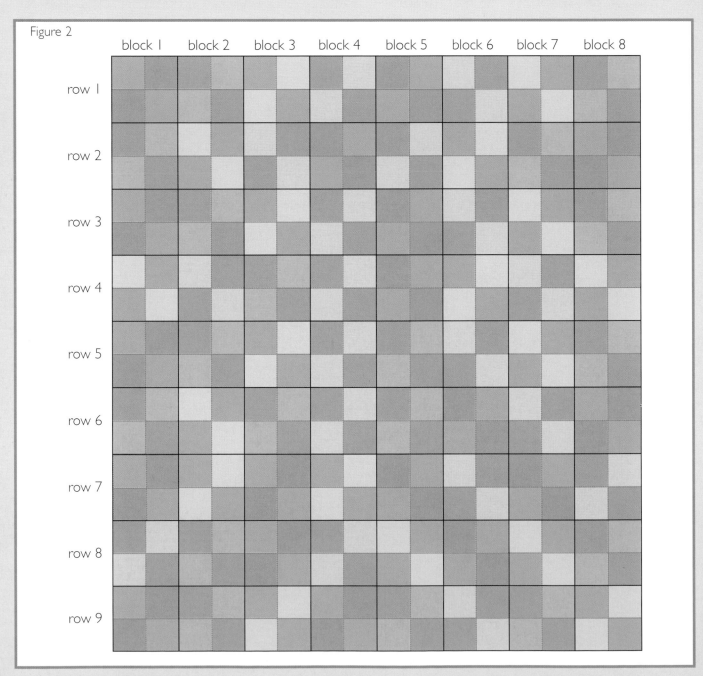

Figure 2

blocks. Press seams to the right. Repeat with the second row, but this time press seams to the left. Continue sewing and pressing the seams in alternate directions until you have completed all nine four-patch rows.

6. With right sides together and matching seam allowances, sew the nine rows together. Press seams downward. (See Figure 2 on page 32)

Assemble the quilt

1. Press the backing fabric.

2. Lay the backing fabric on a flat clean surface, right side down. Center the quilt batting on top of the backing fabric, smoothing out any folds as you go. Center the patchwork top, right side up, on the batting to form a sandwich. Smooth out any folds in the layers. (See Photo B)

Photo B

3. Starting in the center of the quilt, baste the layers together with safety pins or sewing thread. Continue basting outward from the

center in all directions, spacing basting stitches or pins 6"–8" apart. (See Photo C)

Photo C

Tie the quilt

1. Begin at the center of the quilt top at the intersection of four patchwork squares. Use a large eyed sewing needle threaded with mercerized thread to stitch straight down through all three layers. Bring needle up in adjoining diagonal square close to first point and pull thread through all layers, leaving a 2" tail at the point where the needle went down. Repeat stitches, and cut thread, leaving a 2" tail at the point where the needle came up. (See Figure 3)

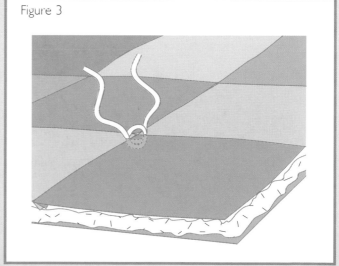

Figure 3

2. Tie the threads together with a square knot to close the top of quilt. (See Figure 4)

3. Tie square knots wherever four squares come together.

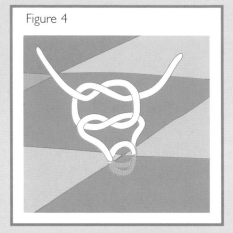

Figure 4

Bind the quilt

1. Baste around quilt ⅛" in from the edge of the patchwork top. Trim backing and batting to ½" beyond patchwork top.

2. Cut four 2⅛" x 44" strips from binding fabric.

3. Fold strips in half lengthwise, wrong sides together, and press. Turn under one long edge of each strip ¼" and press again. Open binding on center fold.

4. With right sides together, pin one binding strip to quilt side, matching unpressed long edge of binding to raw edge of quilt. Repeat with second binding strip on opposite side of quilt.

5. Using sewing machine, sew binding strips to quilt through all layers, taking a ¼" seam allowance. Trim off excess binding.

6. Turn binding over seam allowance and press. Using hand-sewing needle and thread, blind-stitch binding to back of quilt. (See Figure 5) Trim ends of binding to ⅛".

7. Repeat steps 4–6 with remaining binding strips, overlapping the previous bindings at the corners.

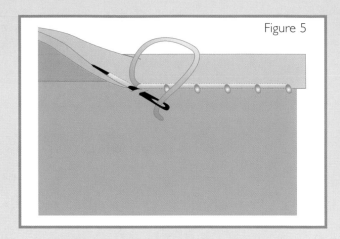

Figure 5

8. With a rotary cutter, trim the ends of the binding, leaving ¼" on each end. Fold the cut ends of the binding over the first binding strips, then fold the binding to the back of the quilt, enclosing all of the cut edges, (See Photo D) and blind-stitch closed. (See Figure 6)

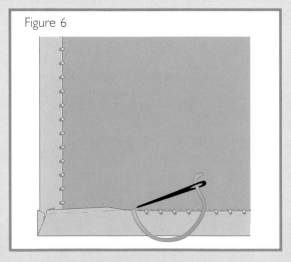

Photo D

Figure 6

How do I appliqué by machine?

Using the zigzag stitch on your sewing machine is a fun and easy way to appliqué pieces and a good technique choice for use on those projects that need to be durable—like the Comfort Tote Bag.

What you need to get started

Fabrics
44"–45"-wide 100% cotton

✂ ¼ yard natural twill canvas for pocket

✂ ¼ yard transfer web

✂ One 3" square each from five fabrics for appliqué

Additional items

☑ Iron

☑ Rotary cutter

☑ Rotary ruler

☑ Scissors

☑ Seam ripper

☑ Sewing machine with a zigzag setting and an open-toed presser foot

☑ Sewing thread

☑ Straight pins

☑ Tote bag with strapping-band handles

Comfort Tote Bag
overall finished size:
15" × 13", excluding handles
Pocket area: 7" × 9"

35

Here's how:

Make the appliqué pocket

1. Cut a 9" x 10" piece from canvas.

2. To make the pocket, finish the top edge of canvas by folding one 9" edge under ¼", fold again ⅜" and press. Topstitch ¼" from folded edge. For bottom edge of pocket, press remaining 9" edge under ¼" and topstitch ⅛" from fold.

3. Refer to Tracing and Transferring Patterns on page 16. On the transfer web, mark five 3" squares. Center and trace a full-sized *reversed* letter within each square. (See Tote Template Patterns on page 37)

4. Cut squares apart and press lettered squares onto the wrong side of the appropriate fabric, following manufacturer's instructions. Cut out each letter.

5. Remove paper backing from each letter and artfully overlap letters to read "MY BAG" on the front of the pocket. Pin in place. (See Photo A)

Photo A

6. Beginning with "MY," remove enough pins from the M to fold it far enough back to expose all of the Y. Remove pins from the Y, press to adhere to canvas.

7. Stitch around Y, using a close zigzag setting. (See Photo B)

8. Fold the M back in place, press and zigzag in place. (See Photo C)

9. Repeat pressing and zigzagging for "BAG" beginning with the bottom letter.

Assemble the tote bag

1. Open side seams of bag to make sewing easier. Lay pocket over front of tote bag and mark desired position with pins.

2. Remove stitching on both inside edges of strapping in pocket area approximately ½" above and below pocket. Insert the raw edges of the pocket under strapping bands. Pin in place.

3. Sew bottom of pocket to bag. (See Photo D)

Photo D

4. Sew strapping edge back down over pocket sides and resew side seams of bag. (See Photo E)

Photo E

Tote Template Patterns

Design Tip: *Another way to apply the pocket is to appliqué it to the bag in much the same way that you added the letters to the pocket. If using this method, finish only the top of the pocket and stitch the pocket's three raw edges down on the bag.*

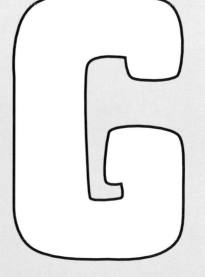

3
technique

What you need to get started

Fabrics
44"–45"-wide 100% cotton

- ✂ ¼ yard gold marble for stripes
- ✂ ¼ yard rust marble for stripes
- ✂ ¼ yard ultrahold fusible web
- ✂ ¾ yard brown marble for binding and backing
- ✂ Quilt batting

Additional items
- ☑ Colored pencil
- ☑ Iron
- ☑ Lead pencil
- ☑ Quilter's ruler
- ☑ Rotary cutter and mat
- ☑ Safety pins
- ☑ Scissors
- ☑ Sewing machine
- ☑ Sewing thread

How do I machine-quilt the layers?

Machine quilting is a good choice for this Falling Leaves Place Mat that will be laundered frequently. This form of quilting is sturdy and adds stability to the quilted piece. In this simple technique, you don't even mark a quilting path. You can "Stitch in the Ditch!" This method can be applied to numerous quilt projects. Be certain to place quilting stitches right along the seam line if possible. This piece minimizes the quilt threads and accents the patchwork.

Here's how:

Make the patchwork top

Refer to What do I need to know about fabrics? on page 14.

1. Cut 13 1½" x 17" fabric strips: seven strips from rust marble and six strips from gold marble.

2. With right sides together, alternately stitch rust and gold strips together lengthwise, taking a ¼" seam allowance, and beginning and ending with a rust strip.

3. Press seams toward rust strips. Press front flat. Trim patchwork top to a width of 16½". (See Figure 1 on page 39)

Falling Leaves Place Mat finished size: 19" x 15"

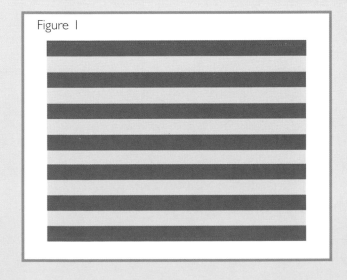

Figure 1

Assemble the place mat

1. Cut one 17" x 21" piece from brown for backing and one 17" x 21" piece from quilt batting.

2. On a clean flat surface, lay brown backing right side down and cover with batting. Center patchwork top, right side up, over backing and batting. Align layers and pin.

3. Sew layers together on the gold side of the seam, using the "Stitch in the Ditch" method. Place your quilting stitches as close as possible to

the patchwork seams—right along the seam line if possible. It's a good idea to use the seam as a guide. (See Photo A)

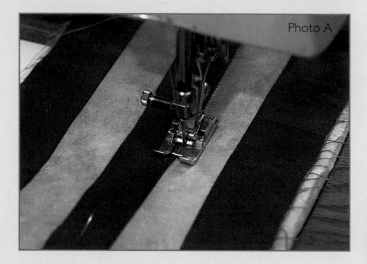

Photo A

4. Machine-bastc along the edges, taking a ¼" seam allowance.

5. Trim the batting/backing to 1¼" beyond the patchwork-top edges.

Bind the place mat

1. Cut four strips from brown fabric: two 3⅝" x 20" strips and two 3⅝" x 24" strips.

2. With wrong sides together, press brown binding strips in half lengthwise, then press one long edge under ¼" on each binding strip.

3. With a lead pencil, mark a dot ¼" in from each corner of the patchwork top. (See Figure 2)

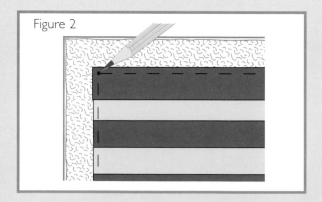

Figure 2

4. With right sides together, center one 20" binding strip on the left edge of place mat top, matching unfolded raw edge of strip to raw edge of place mat. Binding should extend approximately 2½" beyond edge of top. Sew strip to place mat, taking ¼" seam allowance, and stopping at the marked dot. Backstitch several stitches from the dot. Repeat with remaining 20" strip on opposite side. (See Photo B)

Photo B

5. Transfer dot marking to binding. Fold and press binding ends at a 45° angle from marked dot; pin out of the way.

6. Center and pin 24" top and bottom bindings to place mat. Sew bindings, stopping at marked dots. Fold and press binding ends at 45° angle.

7. To make the double-mitered corner, pin overlapping bindings together, matching center fold lines, raw edges, and pressed edges. (See Figure 3 on page 41)

8. On top binding, draw a line from end of seam (marked dot) to the folded edges (a) of

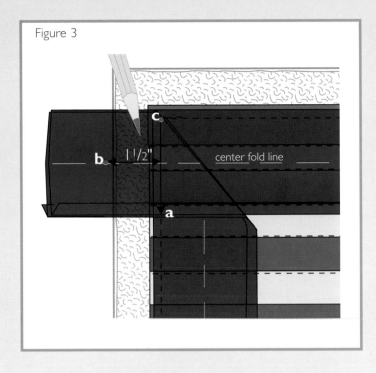

Figure 3

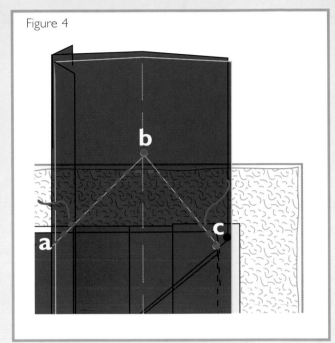

Figure 4

bindings. From this line, measure 1½" along center fold line of binding (finished binding width), and mark (b) with a dot. Draw lines connecting points (a) to (b) and (b) to the original dot (c).

9. Holding binding together at (a), pull binding away from patchwork, then stitch from (a) to (b) to (c), flattening the point at (b) slightly. (See Figure 4) Repeat for remaining three corners. Trim ends ¼" from seams.

10. Fold binding to back. Press, pin, and blind-stitch to the back.

Finish the place mat

1. Refer to Tracing and Transferring Patterns on page 16. Trace 21 leaves with a lead pencil

    Leaf Template Pattern

onto paper side of fusible web. Following manufacturer's instructions, fuse leaves to all three fabrics. Cut out leaves, remove paper backing and fuse to place mat. (See Photo C)

Photo C

41

4
technique

What you need to get started

Fabrics
44"–45"-wide 100% cotton

✂ ⅛ yard light values,
¼ yard dark values, and
¼ yard medium values, for
patchwork top

✂ ¾ yard for backing and
binding

✂ 15" x 40" high-loft
batting

Additional items
☑ Iron

☑ Marking chalk

☑ Quilter's ruler

☑ Quilting thread

☑ Rotary cutter and mat

☑ Safety pins

☑ Scissors

☑ Sewing machine

☑ Sewing thread

☑ Straight pins

Watercolors Table Runner
finished size: 14" x 38"

How do I choose colors?

For the Watercolors Table Runner, choose colorful floral prints at a 1"–2" scale to fit the patchwork squares and have some fun choosing and cutting out the flower faces you'll want in your table runner. Color values are key here—more important even than the colors themselves.

Here's how:

Refer to What do I need to know about fabrics? On page 14.

Make the patchwork top

Refer to What do I need to know about quilt tops? On page 17.

1. Cut a total of 133 2½" squares from floral prints: 25 light-colored values, 53 medium-colored values, and 55 dark-colored values.

2. Arrange the squares on clean flat surface, putting the lightest square in the center and the next three lightest squares on either side of it to form one row of seven light squares. (See Figure 1 on page 43)

3. Continue working outward from the center, light to dark, until you have nine rows of seven squares on either side of the central square. Relax the focus of your eyes a bit to help you see the values of the colors, rearrange any of the squares that stand out of the value order. (See Photo A)

4. Beginning on the left side, sew one row of seven squares together from top to bottom, taking a ¼" seam allowance. Press the seams down-

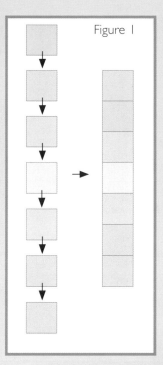

Figure 1

ward. Repeat for the second row, but press seams upward. As you sew each new row, press the seams in alternate directions until

Photo A

you've completed all of the 19 rows. (See Photo B)

Photo B

5. Starting on the left side, sew the rows together. Use straight pins to match seam lines as you go. Press these seams in one direction. (See Figure 2)

Assemble the table runner

1. Cut 15" x 40" piece from backing fabric. Press the backing fabric.

2. Lay the backing fabric on a flat clean surface, right side down. Center the quilt batting on top of the backing fabric, smoothing out any folds in the batting as you go. Center the runner top right side up on the batting to form a sandwich. Smooth out any folds in the layers. Pin layers together in the center and at the four corners, using straight pins.

Hand-quilt the table runner

1. Refer to Baste Stitch on page 25. Starting in the center of the quilt, baste the layers together with sewing thread, using a diagonal baste stitch. Baste from top to bottom and side to side.

2. Refer to Quilt Stitch on page 26. Using a quilt stitch and quilting thread, quilt diagonally across every other square. Remove basting stitches.

Stitching Tip: *Stitching on the bias of your fabric can cause more "give" than when you stitch on the straight grain. Be certain to alternate the*

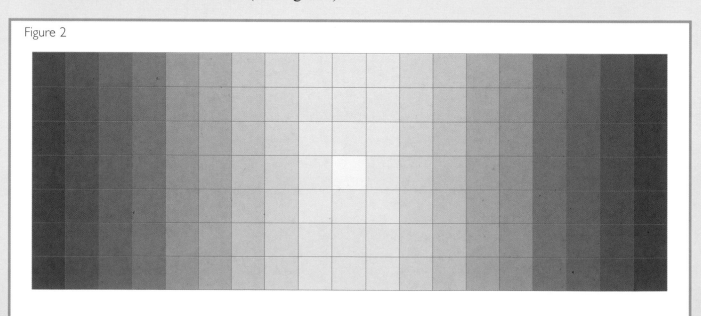
Figure 2

direction in which you are quilting. For example, work down, top left to bottom right, then return up, bottom right to top left. This keeps the fabrics from moving in the single direction of the quilt stitches and distorting your finished piece.

3. Baste layers together just outside the ¼" seam allowance. Trim batting and backing to ⅛" beyond patchwork top to create a ⅜" seam allowance on the outside of the table runner.

Bind the table runner

1. Using a quilter's ruler and marking tool, mark and cut three 1½" fabric strips, the width of the fabric.

2. With right sides together, sew the short ends of strips together to create one continuous binding piece. Sew ends on the diagonal to reduce bulk. (See Figure 3) Trim seam allowances to ¼" and press open. Your binding should now measure more than 112" long.

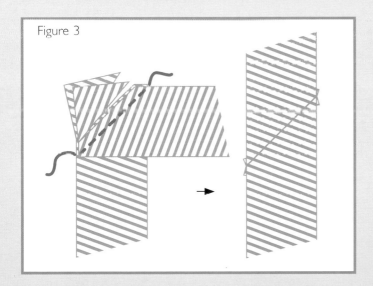

Figure 3

3. With wrong sides together, fold binding in half lengthwise and press. Fold one raw edge under ⅜" and press.

4. On the right side of the table runner, pin binding on one long edge approximately 10"

from a corner. Fold one short end of binding under on a 45° angle so short raw edge of binding meets raw edge of table runner. Pin binding along edge to first corner. Taking a ⅜" seam allowance, stitch to corner, stopping ⅜" from end and backstitching. (See Figure 4)

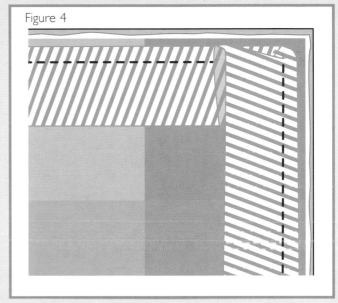

Figure 4

5. Fold binding, wrong sides together, away from table runner at a 45° angle, then fold back down, right sides together, at a right angle to the stitched edge, and align raw edges. Pin and sew to next corner, taking ⅜" seam allowance, stopping and backstitching ⅜" from corner. Repeat for remaining corners and edges, stopping approximately 3" before you reach the beginning of the binding.

6. Pin binding over the starting point, continuing past point until binding overlaps starting point by approximately 1½". Stitch overlap area and trim off excess binding.

7. Refer to Mitered-corner Bindings on page 27. Press binding away from quilt. As you turn the corners, tuck the excess binding fabric under at a 45° angle to create a folded mitered corner. Continue hand-stitching around the entire edge.

How do I make a quilt using templates?

What you need to get started

Fabrics

44"–45"-wide 100% cotton

✂ ⅛ yard country-blue print

✂ ¼ yard antique-gold print

✂ ¼ yard brick-red print

✂ 100% cotton batting

Additional items

☑ ¾"-wide masking tape

☑ 1"-diameter plastic ring

☑ 5"-square clear acetate or plastic

☑ Iron

☑ Large crewel needle

☑ Lead pencil

☑ Permanent fine-point marker

☑ Quilter's ruler

☑ Rotary cutter and mat

☑ Scissors

☑ Sewing machine

☑ Sewing thread

☑ Straight pins

The House Pot Holder is a charming, functional project that helps you practice piecing a traditional quilt motif, while getting the feel of working with multiple layers of batting and binding. And, with the right choice of fabrics, you won't "burn the house down!"

Here's how:

Fabric Tip: 100% cotton fabric and batting is the choice for this potentially flammable quilt project. While cotton will burn, it will not melt or flame up—important considerations for a pot holder. Multiple layers of cotton batting keep heat away from hands, and a double-fold binding reinforces the edges of this heavy-use item.

House Template Patterns

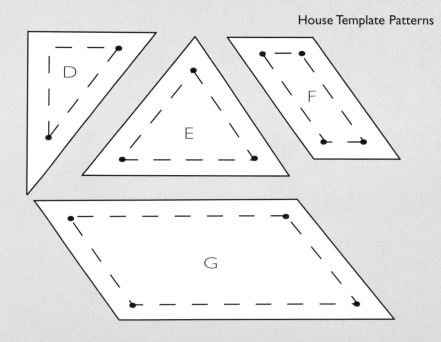

House Pot Holder finished size: 8¼" sq

Make the patchwork top

1. With a permanent fine-point marker, trace tracking templates D, E, F, and G onto clear plastic and cut out. (See House Template Patterns on page 46) *Note: Measurements include ¼" seam allowance.* Using a large crewel needle, punch holes at the corners where the seam allowances meet. (See Photo A on page 48)

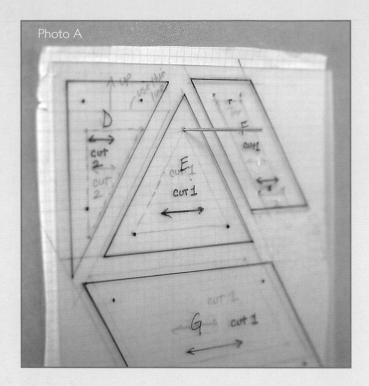

Photo A

2. Referring to Figure 1 and the Cutting Guide, cut out fabrics. Use the template patterns to cut out the angled pieces. Transfer the seam allowance marks to the wrong side of fabric pieces with a pencil through the corner holes.

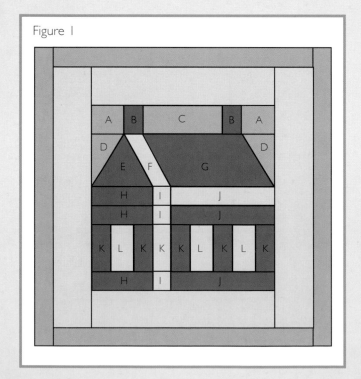

Figure 1

Cutting Guide

Country-blue Print

- Cut two 1¼" x 1⅜" strips for "A" pieces.
- Cut one 1¼" x 2⅝" strip for "C" piece.
- Cut two "D" pieces, using template D; one right and one left.

Brick-red Print

- Cut one piece each from templates "E" and "G."
- Cut three 1" x 2⅛" strips for "H" pieces.
- Cut two 1" x 3¼" strips for "J" pieces.
- Cut five 1" x 1¾" strips for "K" pieces.

Antique-gold Print

- Cut one "F" piece, using template.
- Cut three 1" squares for "I" pieces.
- Cut one 1" x 1¾" strip for "K" piece.
- Cut three 1⅛" x 1¾" strips for "L" pieces.

3. Assemble the pieces as shown in Figure 2.

4. Beginning at row 1, sew pieces, right sides together, taking a ¼" seam allowance. Press seams in the direction indicated by the arrows in Figure 2.

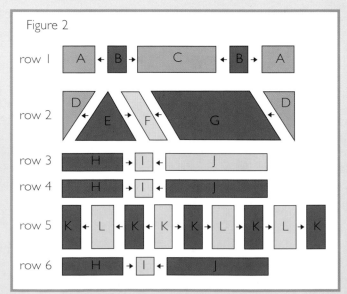

Figure 2

row 1
row 2
row 3
row 4
row 5
row 6

5. Sew row 2 pieces, right sides together, matching marked seam allowance dots to get accurate points. Press seams in direction of arrows and trim points.

6. Continue sewing pieces together into rows; then sew rows together, matching seam allowances. (See Figure 2 on page 48) Press seams toward top. Square and trim.

7. For first border, cut two 1½" x 5⅞" strips and two 1½" x 6⅞" strips from the antique-gold print fabric.

8. With right sides together, sew shorter strips to top and bottom edges of block, taking a ¼" seam allowance. Press seams outward. Repeat for side borders, overlapping top and bottom borders. (See Photo B)

Photo B

9. For second border, cut two 1" x 7⅞" strips and two 1" x 8⅞" strips from blue fabric. Again, beginning with the top border, sew blue border to patchwork as for the gold border. Press and square the patchwork top.

Machine-quilt the potholder

1. Cut a 9" square from gold fabric for backing. Cut 2–3 9"-square pieces from batting. Lay backing fabric, right side down, on a flat surface and center layers of batting on top of wrong side. Baste layers together.

2. Align one edge of a strip of masking tape on the diagonal center of patchwork top. Machine-quilt along both sides of tape, alternating the direction of stitching to avoid distortion. Reposition tape exactly one tape width from stitched quilt line and stitch another line. Continue repositioning and stitching until you reach an outside corner, then repeat on the other side.

3. Trim batting/backing layer even with the patchwork top.

Bind the pot holder

1. Refer to How do I bind a quilt? on page 26. Cut a 2" x 38" strip from red fabric. Fold strip in half lengthwise, wrong sides together, and press. Cut strip into quarters. Press one side of each binding edge up ¼".

2. Beginning at one corner, pin edge of one binding strip to front bottom edge of pot holder, right sides together, and matching raw edges. Sew layers together, taking ¼" seam allowance. Trim binding ends even with quilted top edges.

3. Repeat with another binding strip on the top front edge. Turn bindings over seam allowance and press. Refer to Blind Stitch on page 26. Fold bindings to back of pot holder and attach with blind stitch.

4. Sew remaining two binding strips to sides of pot holder, overlapping previous bindings. Trim ends of binding, leaving ⅜" extending on each of the sides.

5. Fold trimmed ends of binding from front to back over first binding strips, then fold binding to back of pot holder, enclosing all cut edges. Attach with blind stitch.

6. Stitch a plastic ring to the back of one corner.

What you need to get started

Fabrics
44"–45"-wide 100% cotton

- ✂ ⅓ yard black for purse back and lining

- ✂ ⅓ yard rust for quilt top

- ✂ 1¾ yards black twisted-rayon cord, ³⁄₁₆" wide

- ✂ 10" x 20" ultrathin batting

Additional items

- ☑ 10" x 13" rose-patterned quilt stencil

- ☑ Iron

- ☑ Masking tape

- ☑ Quilter's ruler

- ☑ Quilting hoop

- ☑ Quilting needle

- ☑ Quilting thread (black)

- ☑ Scissors

- ☑ Sewing machine

- ☑ Sewing thread

- ☑ Straight pins

- ☑ White marking pencil

How do I hand-quilt stenciled designs?

The quilting itself is the star in the Quilted Envelope Purse. Often referred to as whole-cloth quilting, this form of quilting uses the whole cloth—not pieced. A stencil makes it easy to mark intricate or repetitive designs. We chose a rose design, but a wide variety of precut quilting stencils are available.

Here's how:

Fabric Tip: Choose a solid color to show off the quilt stitches.

Stencil Tip: To make your own stencil from a pattern, simply place plastic over a pattern and trace with a permanent marker. Use a craft knife to cut narrow slits along traced lines just wide enough for your marking tool to contact the fabric below.

Quilt the purse top

1. Cut three 10" x 20" pieces: one from black fabric, one from rust fabric, one from batting.

2. To plan the quilt design, lay rust fabric right side up on hard, flat surface. With the white pencil, mark an outline representing the outer seam allowance of the purse: 17½" x 8". Center the outline on the fabric approximately 1" inside the raw edges. Mark the horizontal and vertical center lines. (See Figure 1 on page 51)

3. Position the stencil along the marked outline to see how the design repeat will work over the length of the marked area. Determine the desired starting point of the design and position the stencil at one end and center side to side.

Quilted Envelope Purse finished size: 8" × 6¼" (folded)

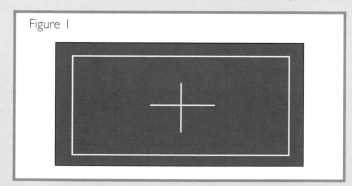

Figure 1

Photo A

4. Transfer lines to fabric with white pencil. Slide stencil to continue the pattern, matching previous lines. (See Photo A) Remove the

stencil and connect all the lines to make them continuous.

5. Lay the black fabric on a clean flat surface, right side down. Center quilt batting over top of black fabric. Center stenciled fabric, right side up, over the batting to form a sandwich. Smooth out any folds in the layers. Pin layers together in the center and at the four corners.

6. Refer to Quilt Stitch on page 26. Use a long baste stitch to baste the layers together, working outward from the center in a grid spaced 2" apart. (See Photo B)

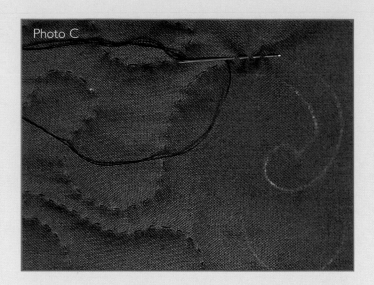

Photo C

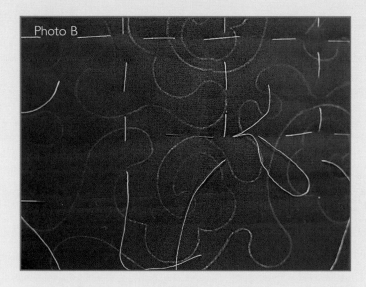

Photo B

7. Place fabric in quilting hoop. Refer to Quilting by Hand on page 24. With black quilting thread, stitch the design in short even quilt stitches. (See Photo C) Remove basting threads.

Assemble the envelope purse

1. Trim the purse top to 8½" x 18", centering quilted design. Measure down 12" on both long sides of quilted top and use pins to mark handle placement.

2. Secure raw ends of twisted cord with tape. Position taped ends at pins, with ends extending ¼" beyond raw edges at sides. Loop excess cord and pin out of the way in center of quilted top.

3. Cut one 6½" x 8½" piece and one 8½" x 12½" piece from selected lining fabric.

4. Fold one short edge of larger lining piece under ¼" and press. Fold under again ¼" and sew. Repeat with one long edge of smaller lining piece.

5. With right sides together, pin smaller lining piece to bottom edge of quilted top, and larger lining piece to top edge, matching raw edges. Sew around outside edges, taking ¼" seam allowance.

6. Trim corners and turn right sides out through lining opening. Press, then blind-stitch the opening closed.

7. Fold lower third of purse up at handle insertion points along lining seam. Pin folded section in place and blind-stitch both sides closed, securing top edge with extra stitches.

8. Beginning at insertion point, stitch cord along each side to cover seams. Continue to edge of purse opening, securing at edge with extra stitches.

Note: If desired, shorten the handle length with an overhand knot. (See Photo A on page 51)

How do I use foundation piecing?

The technique used in the double-sided Christmas Tree Ornament is a relatively modern technique that can be very useful when working on small pieces. Fabric pieces are sewn directly onto a foundation, on which the pattern lines have been drawn, eliminating the need to match points and seams.

What you need to get started

Fabrics
44"–45"-wide 100% cotton

✂ ¼ yard lightweight muslin for foundation

✂ Scraps of one medium brown for patchwork and three differing values of green

Additional items

☑ 7" green satin ribbon, ¹⁄₁₆"-wide

☑ Iron

☑ Pencil

☑ Photocopier

☑ Quilter's ruler

☑ Quilting thread

☑ Scissors

☑ Sewing machine

☑ Sewing threads, coordinate values with fabrics

☑ Straight pins

☑ Transfer paper

☑ Two ⅝" gold star buttons

Christmas Tree Ornament (double-sided) finished size: 4" sq

Here's how:

Fabric Tips: *The fabric pieces can be rough-cut. They need not be exact because you will be sewing on the drawn seam line.*

Quilting Tips: *Each piece is positioned on the back side of the foundation pattern shape, and sewn on the right side. For best results, follow the order given on the pattern. As you finish a piece, it is flipped up and the next piece added. The foundation fabric becomes part of the finished work.*

Make the patchwork top

1. Cut two 5½" squares from muslin. Enlarge Tree Template Pattern 200%. Refer to Tracing and Transferring Patterns on page 16. Trace pattern and transfer it onto a muslin square. Flip the pattern over and transfer a mirror image onto the second muslin square. (See Photo A)

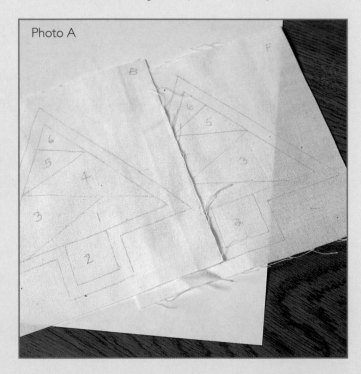

Photo A

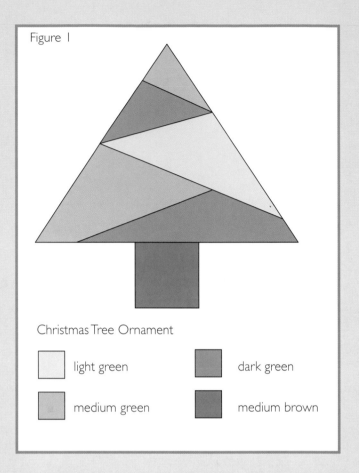

Figure 1

Christmas Tree Ornament

| | light green | | dark green |
| | medium green | | medium brown |

Tree Template Pattern, enlarge 200%

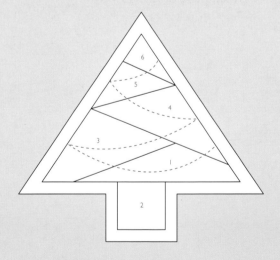

2. Refer to Figure 1. Cut out colored fabric pieces ¼" (or more) larger on all sides than the shapes on the Tree Template Pattern. You need not cut perfect patterns. You can use odd-shaped scraps as long as they are large enough to cover the shape with ¼" to spare on all sides. (See Photo B on page 55)

Photo B

5. Turn the muslin to traced wrong side and sew on the seam allowance between shape 1 and shape 2, starting and stopping a few stitches beyond shared seam allowance. (See Photo C at left) Trim seam allowance to ¼". Turn muslin to right side and press piece 1 away from piece 2. (See Photo D)

Photo D

3. Place one foundation muslin square so that the traced lines (wrong side) face up. Begin piecing fabrics in the order indicated by the numbers on the Tree Template Pattern on page 54. Position fabric piece 1 under shape 1 on the muslin, with the wrong side of piece 1 against the untraced side (right side) of the muslin. Check position by holding fabrics up to a light source. Piece 1 should extend ¼" or more beyond shape 1 on muslin. Pin.

4. Place piece 2 over piece 1, right sides together. Double-check that piece 2 will cover its muslin shape, then pin fabrics to muslin on shared seam allowance between shape 1 and shape 2.

6. Turn foundation back to wrong side and fold muslin back on seam allowance between shape 1 and shape 3 to expose excess fabric of piece 1. Trim piece 1 to ¼" beyond fold. (See Photo E)

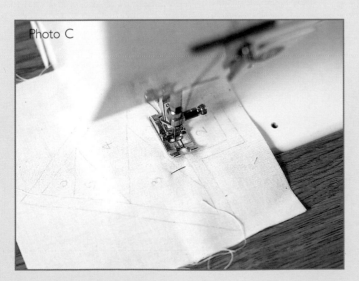

Photo C

Photo E

55

7. Place piece 3 over piece 1, with right sides together, aligning one edge of piece 3 with trimmed edge of piece 1. Double-check placement of piece 3, turn to wrong side and sew on seam line between shape 1 and 3, starting and stopping a few stitches beyond shared seam line. Trim seam allowance to ¼". Turn to right side and press piece 3 away from piece 1. (See Photo F)

8. Turn foundation back to wrong side and fold muslin back on seam line between shape 1, shape 3, and shape 4 to expose excess fabrics of previously sewn pieces 1 and 3. Trim fabric of pieces 1 and 3 to ¼" beyond fold.

9. Place piece 4 over pieces 1 and 3, with right sides together, and proceed as for previous pieces. Repeat the sequence for remaining fabric pieces, following the numerical order shown on pattern.

10. Repeat entire piecing process on mirror image for ornament back.

Assemble the ornament

1. Trim both patchwork pieces along outside cut lines on muslin fabric. (See Photo G)

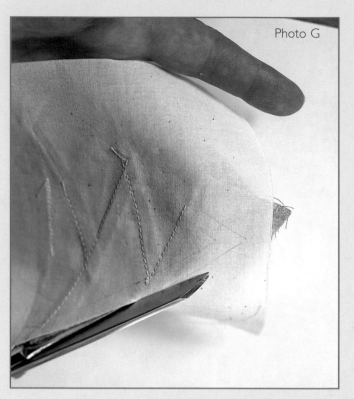

Photo G

2. Fold ribbon in half. Tack ends to top right side of tree at seam allowance. Pin ribbon loop to top of tree.

3. With right sides together, sew the two trees together, taking a ¼" seam allowance and leaving a 1½" opening along one side. Trim points, clip inside corners close to stitching, turn ornament right side out and press. Blind-stitch opening closed.

Quilt the ornament

1. Refer to Quilting by Hand on page 24. Referring to the red quilt lines on the Tree Template Pattern on page 54, hand-quilt through all layers.

2. As a finishing touch, sew two star buttons to tree top at base of ribbon hanger.

How do I make perfect corners with paper piecing?

No matter how accurate you are, perfect corners are challenging. The Amish Star Box Top has plenty of corners to try your skill—but not your patience! Paper piecing is a variation of foundation piecing that will give you perfectly consistent corners—especially on small quilts.

What you need to get started

Fabrics
44"–45"-wide 100% cotton

✂ ⅛ yard each of dark orange, medium orange, dark pink, medium pink, dark purple, medium purple, and ¼ yard black for patchwork

✂ Lightweight batting

Additional items
☑ 5¾"-square cardboard

☑ 7⅛"-square x 2¼"-high oak box with 5¼" opening

☑ Ballpoint pen

☑ Craft glue

☑ Iron

☑ Quilter's ruler

☑ Rotary cutter

☑ Sewing machine needle, 90/14

☑ Sewing machine with an open-toed presser foot

☑ Sewing thread

☑ Scissors

☑ Straight pins

☑ Tear-away stabilizer

☑ Tracing paper

☑ Tweezers

Amish Star Box Top
finished size: 5¼"sq

Here's how:

Sewing Tips: A rotary cutter is recommended. Sewing precisely on the paper lines and accurately trimming block units will make matching painless. Set sewing machine stitch length to 18–20 stitches per inch and use a larger needle (90/14) to perforate the paper for easy removal later. If making multiple blocks of this pattern, you may need to change needles more often, since the paper will dull the needle.

Make the patchwork top

1. Referring to Figure 1, cut fabric squares to the following sizes. To make triangles, cut the squares in half diagonally.

   - For A pieces, cut two $2\frac{3}{4}$" squares: one medium orange (two triangles), one medium pink (two triangles).

   - For B pieces, cut eight $2\frac{3}{8}$" squares: one dark orange (two triangles), one dark pink (two triangles), one dark purple (two triangles), one medium purple (two triangles), four black (eight triangles).

   - For C pieces, cut four $1\frac{7}{8}$" squares from black fabric; do not cut the squares in half.

2. Trace four copies of the Amish Star Template Pattern onto tracing paper for a basic block. Cut out copied patterns $\frac{1}{2}$" beyond outside line. Transfer the numbers shown in Figure 2 on page 59 onto the patterns. (See Photo A on page 59)

3. To make the first basic block (a pink one), hold the pattern with right side up (traced lines

Amish Star Template Pattern

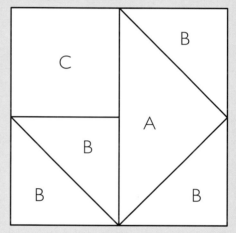

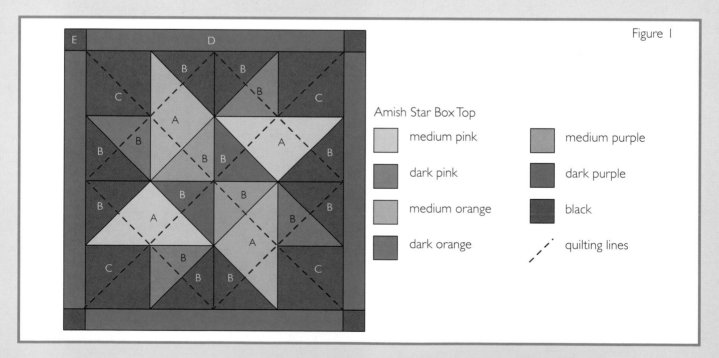

Figure 1

Amish Star Box Top

medium pink	medium purple
dark pink	dark purple
medium orange	black
dark orange	quilting lines

should be large enough to cover paper shape 2 and extend ¼" beyond edges. To double check coverage and position, pin fabrics together on the line between shapes 1 and 2, then flip fabric over to cover shape 2, and view with a lamp. Flip fabric back to proceed.

5. On the traced side of paper, sew on shared seam line between paper shapes 1 and 2. Start and stop approximately ¼" beyond seam line.

6. Fold paper back and trim fabric seam allowance to slightly more than ⅛", using a rotary cutter.

7. Flip piece 2 over shape 2 and press well for perfect points.

8. Turn unit to the wrong side, and pin a medium pink (A) piece, right sides together, over the first two pieces, matching raw edges. Turn paper to the right side and sew on line between shapes 1, 2, and 3. Fold back paper, pulling through extended stitching, and trim seam allowance to ⅛". Flip piece into position and press.

9. Continue placing, sewing, trimming, and pressing in the sequence shown in Figure 3 on page 60, adding each new piece in numerical order to complete block unit. Repeat for a second pink unit. Make two orange units the same way.

10. Keeping the paper on, trim block units. Leave an exact ¼" seam allowance on all sides.

11. Arrange four trimmed blocks as shown in Figure 3.

12. Place two top blocks together and match seams by pinning vertically through both paper and fabric layers at each point and corner. Open to check alignment and pin layers together.

13. Sew on line, beginning and ending at edge of paper and fabric. Press the seam open.

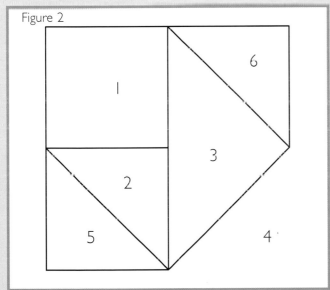

Figure 2

visible) and position a black corner (C) piece, with right side down under the corner pattern shape 1. Be certain there is at least a ¼" seam allowance extending beyond the outline of the shape. Double-check position with a light source, and pin fabric in place.

4. Place a dark pink (B) triangle under the first black square, right sides together. Piece 2

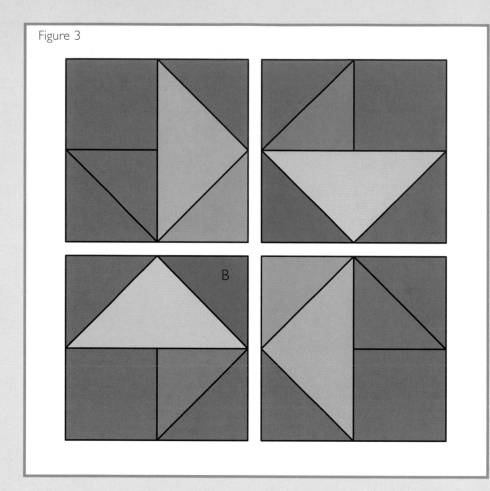

Figure 3

B

Machine-quilt the patchwork top

1. Cut two 5¾" squares, one from batting and one from tear-away stabilizer.

2. Mark quilting lines on the patchwork top as shown in Figure 1 on page 58.

3. Place the patchwork right side down and center batting on wrong side. Center stabilizer on top of batting and pin layers together at corners. Turn patchwork to right side and machine-quilt layers together, following the marked quilting lines. Remove stabilizer.

14. Repeat for bottom two blocks. With paper still attached, sew the top and bottom rows together in the same manner and press seams open.

15. For borders, cut out four 2" x 5" strips from dark purple. Cut four 2" squares from black. Sew two border strips to opposite sides of the patchwork along paper seam line, and press seams toward borders.

16. Sew black corner squares to either end of remaining two strips. Press seams in toward center of strip. Sew these borders to patchwork along remaining edges, carefully matching seam lines. Open and press seam allowances toward border.

17. Remove paper from back of patchwork top, starting at outer edge of block. Use tweezers to remove any paper stuck underneath stitches.

Assemble the box top

1. On the 5¾" cardboard square, mark the vertical and horizontal center. Using basting stitches, mark the centers of the patchwork borders.

2. Matching center markings, position cardboard on wrong side of quilt top. Fold and glue fabric sides to back side of cardboard. Miter fabric corners and clip away excess fabric.

3. Cut an 8½" square from black fabric and glue onto the lightweight cardboard square provided with box. Glue cardboard side of square to the wrong side of quilt top, to cover folded raw edges. Weight glued assembly with heavy books until dry. Insert final assembly into box opening and secure with provided framer's points.

How do I strip-quilt?

The traditional Log Cabin quilt pattern is the essential strip-quilt design. The clever little Log Cabin Pincushion employs the "Stitch and Trim" method, in which the end of the cut strip is sewn to the starting piece, then trimmed to fit. The strip is then repositioned and the stitch-and-trim repeated. This project makes a perfect gift.

What you need to get started

Fabrics
44"–45"-wide 100% cotton

✂ ⅛ yard total of five coordinating prints for patchwork top

✂ Polyester fiberfill

Additional items
☑ Iron

☑ Long needle

☑ Pencil

☑ Quilter's ruler

☑ Scissors

☑ Sewing machine

☑ Sewing thread

☑ Straight pins

Log Cabin Pincushion
finished size:
4½"sq × 2¼"h

Here's how:

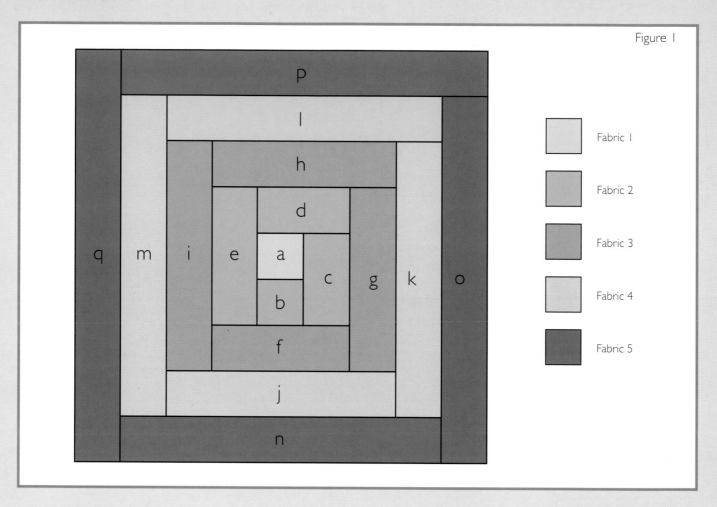

Figure 1

Fabric 1

Fabric 2

Fabric 3

Fabric 4

Fabric 5

Make the patchwork top

1. Cut 1"-wide strips from each of the five different fabrics. (See Figure 1)

   ■ Fabric one: 1" square

   ■ Fabric two: 7" long

   ■ Fabric three: 11" long

   ■ Fabric four: 15" long

   ■ Fabric five: 19" long

2. To begin strip-quilting, position the 1" square of fabric one onto one end of a 7" strip, right sides together. Sew square to strip, taking a ¼" seam allowance. (See Figure 2) Trim strip evenly with

edge of square and press seam allowance away from the center square.

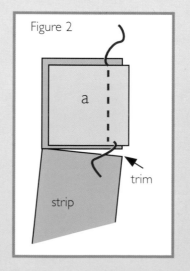

Figure 2

a

trim

strip

3. Rotate sewn unit to the right and position, right sides together, on the end of 7" strip as before, then sew along the right side. Trim the strip even with the unit and press seam toward section B. (See Figure 3 on page 63)

4. Rotate and sew the 7" fabric strip twice more to complete the first border. As you sew, press each seam toward section B. (See Figure 4)

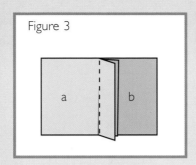

Figure 3

5. Rotate finished unit to the right. Continue to add strips, trimming and pressing as you go. For the second border, use an 11" strip. For the third border, use a 15" strip. For the fourth border, use a 19" strip. Borders will be ½" wide when finished. Trim and square the patchwork top when necessary. (See Figure 5)

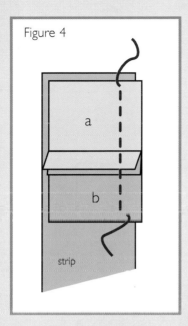

Figure 4

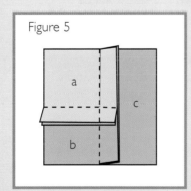

Figure 5

Assemble your pincushion

1. Cut 5" squares from fabrics as follows:
   ■ Fabric one: two squares
   ■ Fabric two: two squares
   ■ Fabric five: one square

2. If necessary, trim all 5" squares to match patchwork top. For top pincushion pillow, sew the patchwork top and fabric five square, right sides together, taking a ¼" seam allowance and leaving a 2" opening in center of one side. Trim corners and turn right side out.

3. Fill pillow moderately full with fiberfill and slip-stitch opening closed.

4. For center and bottom pillows, repeat top pillow construction, using two squares each of fabrics one and two.

5. To tie pillows together, stack pillows with patchwork pillow on top. Thread a long needle with sewing thread and insert needle through bottom pillow approximately 1¼" from one corner. Bring needle straight up through all three pillows, coming out directly under one outside corner of first border of patchwork. Refer to Technique 1, Figure 4 on page 34. Tie with a square knot. Pull stitch to indent pillows. Repeat for ties in remaining corners. (See Photo A)

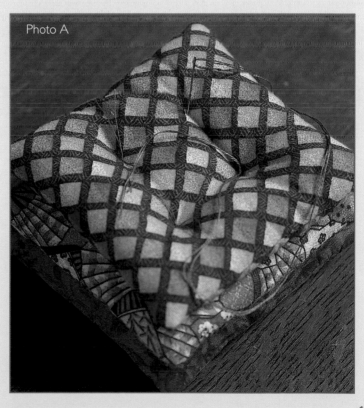

Photo A

Fabrics

44"–45"-wide 100% cotton

✂ ⅛ yard total hand-dyed cotton scraps in blues, browns, greens, and rust-reds for appliqué

✂ ⅓ yard ecru for pillow front

✂ ½ yard red-brown print for pillow back

✂ Medium-weight batting

✂ Polyester fiberfill

Additional items

☑ Embroidery floss, green

☑ Freezer paper

☑ Iron

☑ Needles for appliqué

☑ Pencil

☑ Quilter's ruler

☑ Quilting hoop

☑ Quilting thread, ivory

☑ Scissors

☑ Sewing machine

☑ Sewing threads

☑ Straight pins

☑ Thimble

☑ Tracing paper

☑ Tweezers

How do I hand-appliqué?

The Baltimore Album Quilt Pillow is the ultimate inspiration for hand appliqué, with graceful shapes and beautiful colors. Traditional Baltimore Album quilts were worked with the "needle-turn" method, in which the quilter would turn under the seam allowance with a blind stitch as it was being sewn down. Modern materials, such as freezer paper, have brought time-saving techniques that help beginners' projects look as professional as those of the "old hands."

Here's how:

Appliqué Tips: Freezer paper has a plastic coating on one side that temporarily sticks to fabric when you iron it on, and pulls off easily when you have finished. Press the seam allowance exactly over the edges of the freezer paper and baste it in position for a perfectly finished edge. The parts of the appliquéd piece that will be covered by another piece are not turned under or stitched.

When you need more than one of the same shape, trace the shape onto a separate piece of paper and cut a number of larger freezer paper squares. Staple the freezer paper squares together at the corners and use the tracing to cut out all layers at once.

Make the appliqué top

1. Refer to Tracing and Transferring Patterns on page 16. Trace Baltimore Album Template Patterns A—F on page 69 onto the paper side of the freezer paper. Make one freezer-paper piece for each piece of fabric. (See Figure 1 on page 66) Mark the letters on the pattern pieces with a pencil and cut out patterns.

Baltimore Album Quilt Pillow finished size: 12"sq

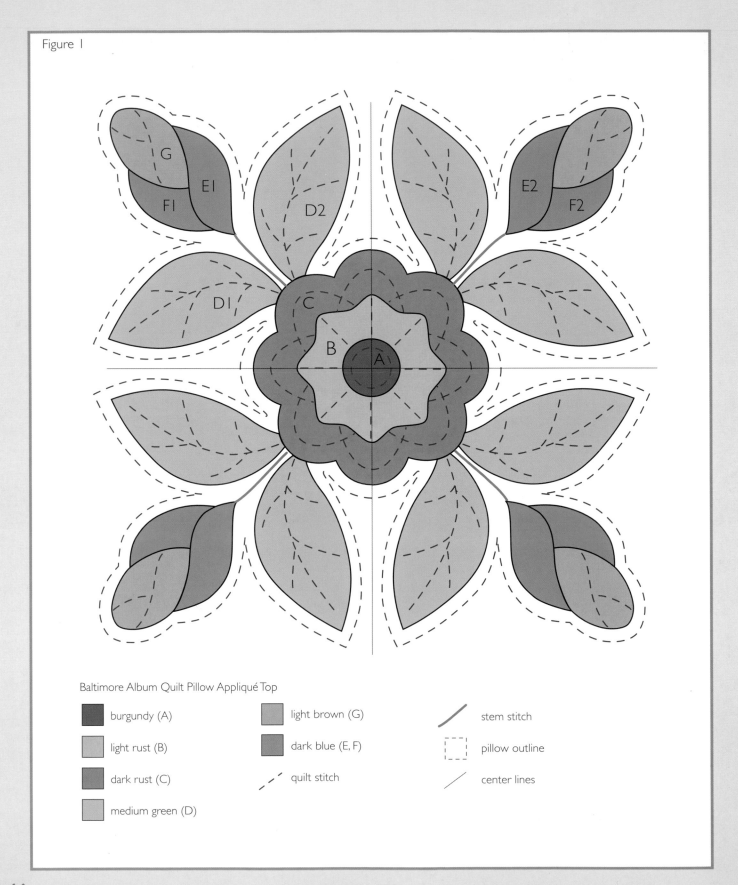

Figure 1

Baltimore Album Quilt Pillow Appliqué Top

- burgundy (A)
- light rust (B)
- dark rust (C)
- medium green (D)
- light brown (G)
- dark blue (E, F)
- quilt stitch
- stem stitch
- pillow outline
- center lines

2. Following the color key in Figure 1 on page 66, lay out paper pieces, plastic side down, on the wrong sides of appropriate fabrics, leaving at least ½" between pieces. Press paper pieces to fabrics, using a medium-hot dry iron on a hard flat surface such as a wooden cutting board.

3. Cut out fabric pieces ¼" beyond edges of paper patterns. (See Photo A)

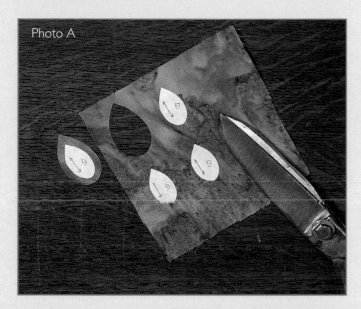

Photo A

4. On wrong side of appliqué pieces, press ¼" seam allowance snugly over edge of paper patterns. (See Photo B) Do not turn edges on

Photo B

sides that will be overlapped by other pieces. Baste seam allowances in place, beginning and ending basting threads on top for easy removal.

5. Cut out one 12" square from ecru fabric. Find the center by folding the fabric into quarters. Lay fabric right side up over appliqué block as in Figure 1 and align center lines with fabric folds. Tape in position. Lightly trace design lines onto right side of ecru fabric, using a pencil.

Photo C

6. Beginning with the leaf pieces (D), pin one appliqué piece at a time over its traced shape on fabric. Refer to Blind Stitch on page 26. With matching color thread, blind-stitch piece to fabric. Do not stitch the unturned edges that will be covered with other appliqué pieces.

7. Continue pinning and stitching the bud pieces (E, F, G) to the ecru fabric, in the sequence they overlap: first G, then F, and finally E. Remove basting stitches. Stem-stitch the buds (See Figure 2) where indicated on Figure 1, using two strands of embroidery floss.

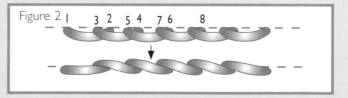

Figure 2

8. Turn to wrong side of design unit to remove freezer paper. For small pieces, make a small bias cut through only the background fabric and pull out paper with tweezers; smooth cut edges down. *Note: Bias cut won't fray.* For large pieces, trim background fabric away, leaving ¼" seam allowance inside the appliquéd shape and remove paper with tweezers.

9. Assemble the flower center before adding it to the ecru fabric as described in the following paragraphs.

    9a. Cut and baste piece A from appropriate fabric as you did for the leaves and buds. Appliqué it in the center of the fabric you will use for piece B. Remove the basting stitches and paper.

    9b. Center paper pattern B over back of piece A (on the wrong side of piece B fabric). Cut and baste piece B. Appliqué it to the center of fabric you will use for piece C. Remove basting stitches and paper.

    9c. Center paper pattern C over back of piece B (on the wrong side of fabric C). Cut and baste piece C, then appliqué it in position on ecru design unit. Remove basting stitches and paper. Press appliquéd top, then blind-stitch top to ecru fabric.

Quilt the appliquéd top

1. Transfer interior quilting lines on leaves and flower (See Figure 1 on page 66) to appliqué top, using tracing paper and pencil. *Note: A white pencil works well for dark colors.* First trace the quilting lines, then position the tracing paper on the appliqué and perforate the traced line with the pencil at regular intervals to create lightly dotted lines on the fabric. Do not trace the quilting lines around the outside of the appliquéd pieces.

2. Cut one 12" square from batting, then baste to wrong side of appliquéd top ½" in from edges.

3. Using a quilt hoop, first quilt the marked interior lines on the leaves and flower. Refer to Outline Quilting on page 25. Complete the quilting by adding an outline ⅛" outside appliquéd edges.

Hand-quilting Tips: Begin in the center of quilt and work outward. Use a hoop to make sure quilt top, batting, and backing are smooth. Work with short lengths of quilter's thread (18"–20" at a time) to minimize fraying. Knot one end. Using a thimble, insert needle into the quilt top and batting approximately ½" from where you wish to begin quilting, preferably in a seam line. Bring needle up at the beginning point; when knot catches on quilt top, give thread a quick, short pull to "pop" knot through fabric into batting.

Holding the needle with your sewing hand and placing your other hand underneath the quilt, use a thimble to push the tip of the needle down through all layers. As soon as the needle touches your finger underneath, use that finger to push the tip of the needle only back up through the layers to top of quilt. (The amount of needle showing above the fabric determines the length of the quilting stitch.) Rock the needle up and down, taking 3–6 stitches before bringing the needle and thread completely through the layers. Check the back of the quilt to be certain stitches are going through all layers. When quilting through a seam allowance or corner, you may need to take one stitch at a time.

Assemble the double-flange pillow

1. With design centered, trim the appliquéd assembly to 11" square. Cut a second 11" square from ecru fabric for backing.

2. With right sides together, pin appliquéd top to backing square. Taking ½" seam allowance, sew around all four sides, leaving a 4" opening centered on one side for turning. Remove pins, trim corners, turn right sides out, and press. Blind-stitch the opening closed.

3. Cut two 13" squares from red-brown print fabric and one 13" square from batting. Baste batting to wrong side of one fabric square. With right sides of fabric squares together, pin layers together with batting on outside. Taking ½" seam allowance, sew around all four sides, leaving a 4" opening centered on one side for turning. Remove pins, trim corners, turn right sides out, then press. Blind-stitch the pillow opening closed.

4. Center and baste appliqué unit on top of fabric unit. Sew units together, 1⅝" inside the ecru edge, leaving a 4" opening centered on one side for stuffing.

5. Stuff pillow with polyester fiberfill, taking care to fill corners. Machine-sew the opening closed.

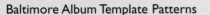

Baltimore Album Template Patterns

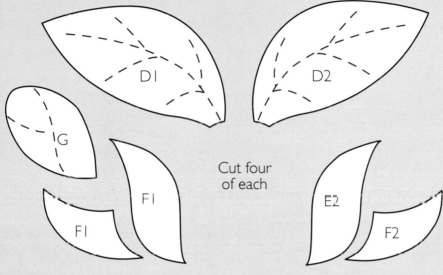

D1

D2

G

F1

Cut four
of each

F1

E2

F2

Cut one of each

A

C

B

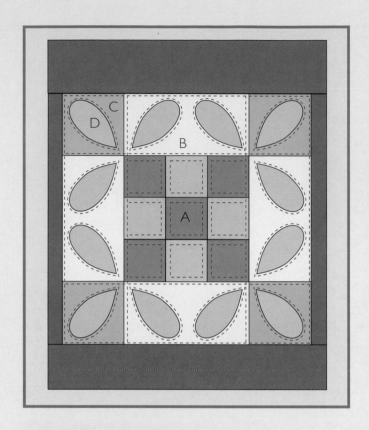

Section 3: Beyond the Basics

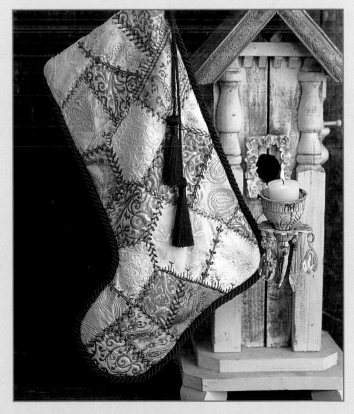

What you need to get started

Fabrics

44"–45"-wide 100% cotton

- ✂ ⅛ yard light gray,
  ⅛ yard medium gray,
  ⅛ yard light red,
  ¼ yard dark gray, and
  ¼ yard medium red for
  patchwork

- ✂ 11" square ultralight batting

Additional items

- ☑ 3" square of clear acetate or plastic
- ☑ Iron
- ☑ Permanent fine-point marker
- ☑ Quilter's ruler
- ☑ Quilting thread
- ☑ Rotary cutter
- ☑ Scissors
- ☑ Sewing machine
- ☑ Sewing thread
- ☑ Straight pins

Card Tricks Coasters
finished size: 5"sq each

How do I make a miniature patchwork using template patterns?

Matching seams and points on small pieces can be challenging, but there are some tips to help you master the skills. These clever Card Tricks Coasters employ a traditional patchwork pattern that uses different colors cut from only two pattern pieces.

Here's how:

Make the patchwork top

1. Refer to Tracing and Transferring Patterns on page 16. Trace Coaster Template Patterns on page 74 onto clear acetate with permanent marker, (See Photo A on page 74) then cut out.

2. Use templates to cut the following number of pieces. For a set of four coasters, multiply the number of pieces for each color by four.

Fabric	Template A	Template B
Dark gray	2	2
Light gray	4	4
Medium gray	2	2
Dark red	2	2
Medium red	2	2

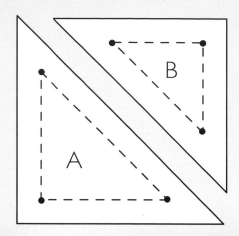

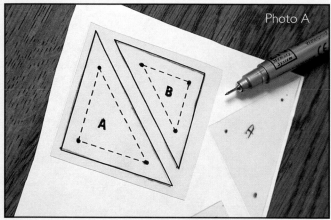

Photo A

3. For each coaster, make nine small unit blocks, taking a ¼" seam allowance. Press seams toward dark colors and trim points flush with raw edges. (See Photo B)

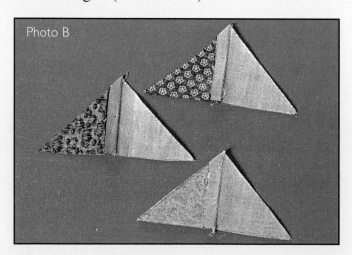

Photo B

3a. Sew a light gray piece A to one of each of the four other piece A colors. (See Figure 1)

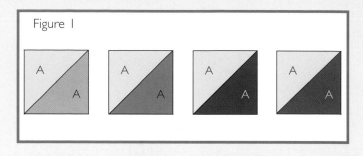

Figure 1

3b. Sew a light gray piece B to one of each of the other four piece B colors. Then sew each of the remaining four A pieces to the assembled B pieces combining the colors as shown in Figure 2.

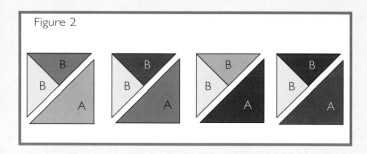

Figure 2

3c. Combine remaining B pieces as shown in Figure 3.

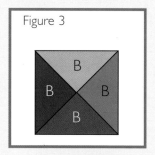

Figure 3

4. Rotate the nine blocks so that they match the positions as shown in Figure 4 on page 75.

5. Sew the three blocks together to form each row. Press each row's seam allowances in one direction, alternating direction for each row. (See Figure 4)

6. Sew three rows together to form a square patchwork top. Press seams away from center. Press top and trim edges, if necessary.

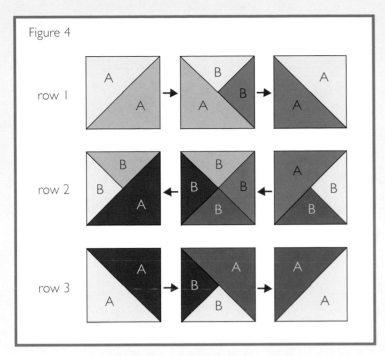

Figure 4

row 1

row 2

row 3

7. For each coaster, cut two 1" x 5½" and two 1" x 4½" strips from medium red or dark gray fabric. *Note: If making four coasters, multiply number of strips by four.*

8. Sew a single short border strip to a side of patchwork top, right sides together and aligning raw edges. Sew second short strip to opposite side. Press seams toward border. Repeat with longer strips on top and bottom.

Assemble the coaster

1. For each coaster backing, cut one 5½" square from fabric used as borders. Cut one 5½" square from batting.

2. Pin batting to wrong side of backing piece. Pin right side of patchwork to right side of backing. Taking a ¼" seam allowance, sew layers together, leaving a 3" opening in the center of one side.

3. Trim corners diagonally, turn coaster right side out, then press. Refer to Blind Stitch on page 26. Use a blind stitch to finish the opening.

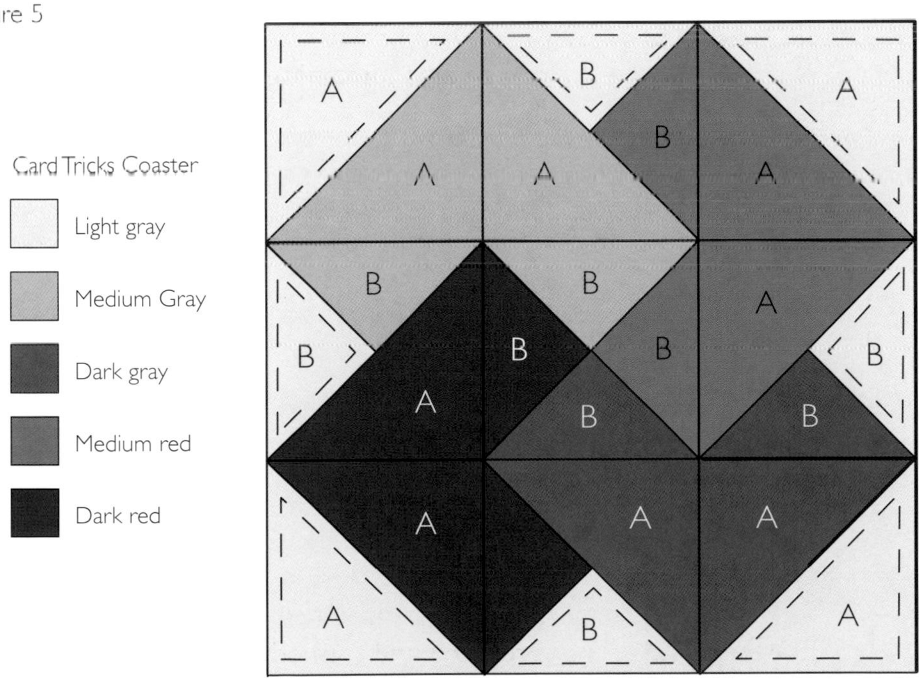

Hand-quilt the coaster

1. Refer to Outline Quilting on page 25. Add a row of outline quilting through all layers, ⅛" from the inside edge of the light gray "A" triangles. (See Figure 5)

Figure 5

Card Tricks Coaster

☐ Light gray

▨ Medium Gray

▨ Dark gray

▨ Medium red

■ Dark red

How do I assemble Seminole patchwork?

What you need to get started

Fabrics

44"–45"-wide 100% cotton rainbow sherbet-colored fabrics

✂ ⅛ yard grape,
⅛ yard peach, and
¼ yard raspberry for patchwork top

✂ 8½"-square lightweight batting

Additional items

☑ Iron

☑ Pencil

☑ Quilter's ruler

☑ Rotary cutter and mat

☑ Scissors

☑ Sewing machine

☑ Sewing thread

☑ Straight pins

The Jewel-toned Eyeglass Case is a treasure of Seminole patchwork. Seminole patchwork is named for the Native Americans known as the Seminoles. They create this beautiful patchwork using the technique we now call strip-quilting. This technique is not traditional, because nothing is actually quilted. But the patchwork is so elegant and simple to construct that it has become an American favorite.

Here's how:

Make the patchwork top

1. Cut fabric strips according to the dimensions listed below:
   - Grape: 1½" x 12½" (center strip)
     ¾" x 10½" (edging strip)

   - Peach: 1½" x 12½" (center strip)
     ¾" x 10½" (edging strip)

   - Raspberry: 1¼" x 12½" (center strip)
     2" x 10½" (edging strip)
     6" x 10½" (edging strip)

Jewel-toned Eyeglass Case finished size: $1\frac{1}{8}$" × $3\frac{3}{4}$" (folded)

2. Assemble three center strips and sew, with right sides together, taking ¼" seam allowance, to form one piece. (See Figure 1)

3. Press seam allowance away from center strip. Measure ten 1¼"-wide increments along the length of sewn strips and cut into ten pieces. (See Figure 2 on page 78)

4. Reassemble the cut pieces as shown in

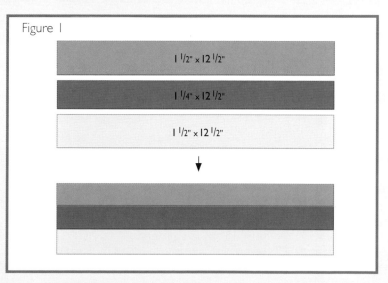

Figure 1

$1\frac{1}{2}$" × $12\frac{1}{2}$"

$1\frac{1}{4}$" × $12\frac{1}{2}$"

$1\frac{1}{2}$" × $12\frac{1}{2}$"

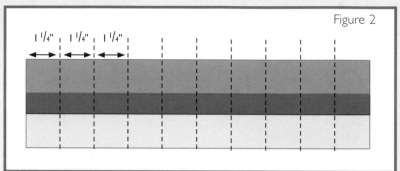

Figure 2

Figure 3 and stitch, taking a ¼" seam allowance. As you go, match bottom seam line of the center strip on the left to top seam line of the center strip on the right. Repeat for all ten pieces. Refer to Technique 9, Step 2 on page 62. Press seams in one direction.

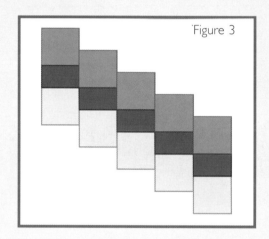

Figure 3

5. With pencil and quilter's ruler, lightly mark a seam line ⅛" outside of center square "points." (See Figure 4) Mark ¼" seam line along one long edge of grape edging strip. Repeat for

peach edging strip. Matching drawn seam lines, pin and sew grape edging strip to side of patchwork with peach fabric. Repeat, sewing peach edging strip to side of patchwork with grape fabric. Trim points from patchwork along raw edge of seam allowance. Press seam allowances toward patchwork.

6. With right sides together, pin one long edge of smaller raspberry strip to grape edging, matching raw edges. Sew, taking ¼" seam allowance. Repeat, sewing remaining larger raspberry strip to peach edging. Press seam allowances away from patchwork.

Assemble the eyeglass case

1. For inside lining, cut 8½" square from raspberry fabric and 8½" square from batting.

2. Lay design assembly flat. Beginning at center of design, measure 2⅛" out to edges of band and 4¼" out to either side. From these points, trim design assembly to 8½" square. (See Figure 5 on page 79)

3. Baste batting to back of design assembly.

4. With right sides together, pin lining to design assembly and sew together, taking ¼" seam allowance. Trim batting from seam allowance and press seams toward lining. Topstitch ⅛" from seam on lining side. (See Figure 6 on page 79)

Figure 4

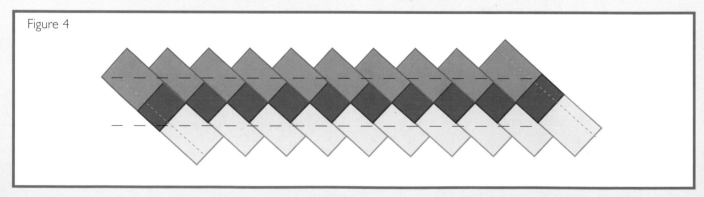

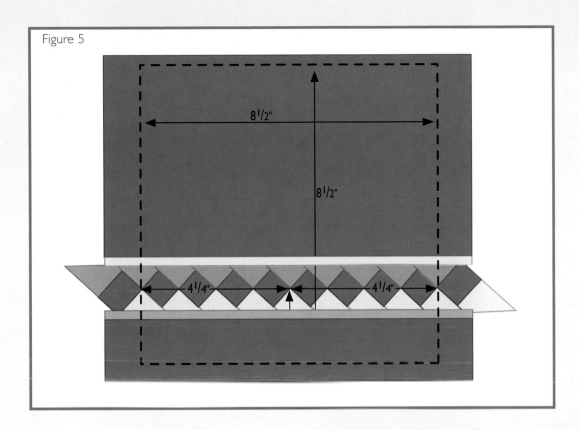

Figure 5

8½"

8½"

4¼"   4¼"

corners, turn the eyeglass case right side out, and blind-stitch opening closed. Then remove visible basting stitches.

7. Use a quilter's ruler to push the lining into the case. Press.

5. Fold in half lengthwise, with right sides together, matching the center seam line. Pin around the three raw edges.

6. Beginning at fold, sew around three raw edges, taking a ¼" seam allowance, leaving a 2" opening on the lining side for turning. (See Figure 7) Refer to Blind Stitch in the Glossary on page 111. Trim seams and

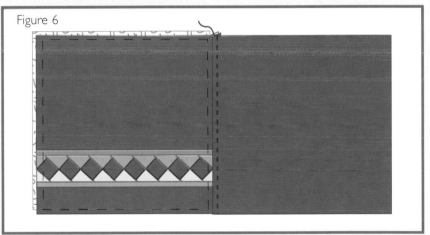

Figure 6

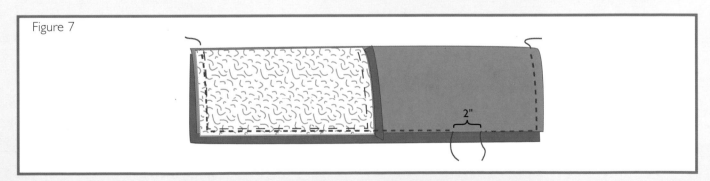

Figure 7

2"

How do I add surface quilt embroidery?

No introduction to quilting would be complete without the beloved crazy quilt. First popularized in Victorian times, the crazy quilts from that era favored the lush velvet, brocade, silk and satin scraps from elegant dresses. But that wasn't enough—in true Victorian "over-the-top" style, they added ornate stitchery at the seam joins. In the case of the Crazy-quilt Stocking, too much of a good thing is truly wonderful!

What you need to get started

Fabrics
44"–45"-wide 100% cotton

- ✂ ⅜ yard medium-weight cream damask, ⅜ yard ivory cotton, and ½ yard white cotton for stocking

- ✂ Assorted elegant scraps (satins, brocades, metallics and damasks) for patchwork top

Additional items

- ☑ 32" of ³⁄₁₆"-diameter antique red cord curtain tieback and tassel

- ☑ 1 yard of ³⁄₁₆"-diameter antique red cord

- ☑ Beading needle #10

- ☑ Brown pattern paper

- ☑ Embroidery hoop

- ☑ Embroidery needle #7

- ☑ Fray preventative

- ☑ Gold seed beads

- ☑ Iron

- ☑ Marking chalk

- ☑ Masking tape

- ☑ Metallic embroidery flosses: gold & red

- ☑ Permanent fine-point marker

- ☑ Pressing cloth

- ☑ Quilter's ruler

- ☑ Scissors

- ☑ Sewing machine with zigzag

- ☑ Sewing thread

- ☑ Straight pins

Crazy-quilt Stocking
finished size: 12¼" × 17¾"

Here's how:

Make the patchwork top

1. Refer to Tracing and Transferring Patterns on page 16. Enlarge Stocking Template Pattern, using the grid as a guide. Trace the enlargement onto a piece of pattern paper with a permanent marker, then cut out pattern.

2. Press the white cotton fabric. With a piece of chalk, transfer stocking outline to the center of the fabric. Draw seam line ⅝" inside the outline. Use bright thread to sew a baste stitch on seam line. (See Photo A on page 82)

3. Cut approximately 25 3"–4" pieces of randomly shaped patches from elegant scraps.

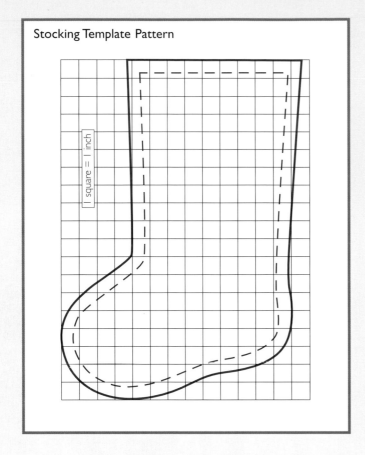

Stocking Template Pattern

1 square = 1 inch

Press out any wrinkles. Starting in upper right corner of stocking, place a patch so that it overlaps the stitched seam line by at least ¼". Place the second patch next to the first, overlapping raw edges by ¼". Trim edges, if necessary, and pin in place. Using a medium zigzag, stitch along overlapped raw edges. (See Photo B)

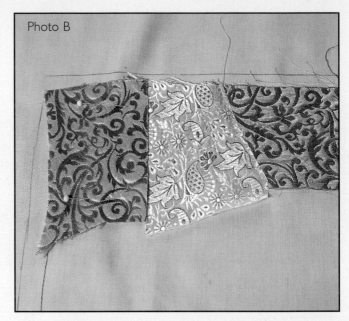

Photo B

4. Continue adding patches until you have filled the stocking shape. Use fray preventative to seal any loose fabric edges.

5. Turn patchwork over and machine-baste just outside thread seam line. Press.

Embroider the patchwork top

1. Position a section of patchwork top in an embroidery hoop. Using three strands of either gold or red metallic floss in 14" to 16" lengths, cover the zigzagged edges with embroidery stitches. (See Embroidery Stitches on page 83) Use two strands to attach beads. To keep stitches even, mark the width of the stitches on either side of the zigzag with pins. Press completed top using a hot iron and a pressing cloth.

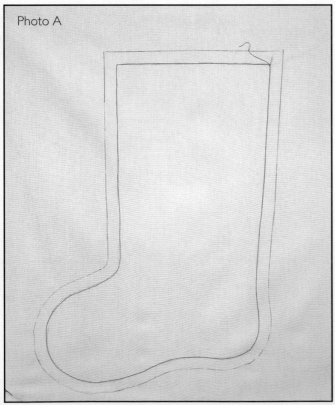

Photo A

2. Trim the entire patchwork top along traced cutting line.

Assemble the stocking

1. Seal cut ends of cord with tape. Beginning at the top of one side, pin cord to right side of patchwork top, aligning raw edges. Baste in place, remove pins.

2. Use stocking pattern to cut out one piece of cream damask fabric (stocking back) and two pieces of ivory fabric (lining).

3. With right sides together, pin stocking back to patchwork top. Taking a ⅝" seam allowance and using a zipper foot to stay close to the cord, sew the layers together, leaving the top edge open.

4. Trim seam allowances to ¼" and clip curves. Turn stocking right side out and press.

5. Sew lining pieces, with right sides together, taking ⅝" seam allowance. Leave the top open. Also leave a 4"–5" opening on one long side.

6. Trim seam allowance to ¼", clip curves. Do not turn.

7. Slip stocking (right sides out) into lining (wrong sides out), and stitch stocking to lining around top edge, taking ⅝" seam allowance.

8. Trim seam allowance and turn right side out through side opening of lining. Blind-stitch opening closed.

9. Tuck lining into stocking. Press stocking.

10. For hanger: Fold tieback cord over with one end 3" longer than the other. Make an overhand knot for the hanger 3" from fold.

11. Sew a hanger knot securely to cord-top at the back of the stocking.

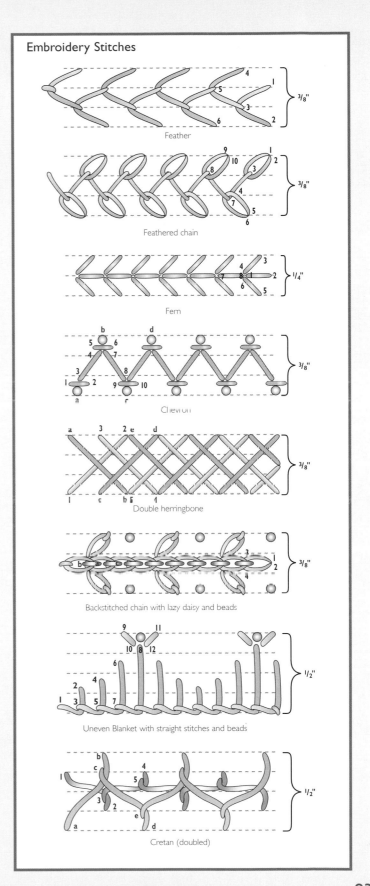

Embroidery Stitches

Feather

Feathered chain

Fern

Chevron

Double herringbone

Backstitched chain with lazy daisy and beads

Uneven Blanket with straight stitches and beads

Cretan (doubled)

4
project

What you need to get started

Fabrics
44"–45"-wide 100% cotton

✂ ⅛ yard dark red (Fabric 5),
⅛ yard red (Fabric 4),
⅛ yard light tan (Fabric 3),
⅓ yard tan (Fabric 2)
for patchwork and backing

✂ ¼ yard ecru (Fabric 1) for embroidery

✂ Lightweight quilt batting

Additional items

☑ ½" wooden dowel (9½")
☑ Embroidery hoop
☑ Embroidery needle
☑ Iron
☑ Quilter's ruler
☑ Red embroidery floss
☑ Rotary cutter
☑ Sewing machine
☑ Sewing thread
☑ Straight pins
☑ Two 1¹⁄₁₆" finial dowel caps

How do I frame needlework with a lattice-strip border?

Redwork was another "quilt fever" that caught quiltmakers' imaginations. In the late 19th century, few domestic items escaped decorative stitchery, and the term "art needlework" was used to distinguish it from plain sewing. At the time, the value of "beauty" was often gauged by its relation to utility, and art needlework took the place of paintbrush and paint. The quilt became the canvas.

The charming illustration for our Redwork Wall Hanging was designed by Sandra Orton. She has selected a strip-quilted lattice border as a framing device.

Here's how:

Notes on Redwork: The redwork style evolved as women traced outlines from whatever caught their fancy, using pen and ink or watercolor. Studies in natural history, animals, birds, children's faces and toys, household items, and sayings can be found on the thousands of antique quilts that remain from this period. They came to be known by a number of names: picture, storybook, Mother Goose, nursery rhyme, or simply pictorial, and were invariably worked in colorfast "Turkey red" cotton floss.

Redwork Wall Hanging finished size: 8¾" × 10¼" including hanging tabs

Make the embroidered center

1. Refer to Tracing and Transferring Patterns on page 16. Cut a 9" square from embroidery fabric, center fabric over Redwork Design on page 88, and lightly trace design in pencil.

2. Refer to Detail of Embroidery Stitches and Listing of Embroidery Stitches on page 88. Use the stitch diagrams on the Redwork Design to embroider the design. Press completed embroidery. Trim fabric to a 5½" square (approximately ¾" beyond design).

Make the patchwork top

1. Cut one 1" x 36" fabric strip from each of the four tan and red fabrics.

2. With right sides together, sew a light red strip to a dark red strip on one long edge, taking ¼" seam allowance. Cut unit into two equal 18" lengths. Repeat for tan strips, sewing dark to light and cutting strip unit in half. Press seam allowances toward darker colors.

3. Rotate strips so the dark strips are toward the inside of one set and toward the outside of the other. (See Figure 1) Sew each of the sets together to make two four-strip units. Cut these in half to make four 9"-long four-strip units. Press.

4. Select one of the patchwork assemblies with the dark strips on the outside. With right sides together, pin the raw edge of the dark red side to the right edge of the embroidery. Beginning at top edge, sew together, taking a ¼" seam allowance, stopping ¼" from bottom edge of embroidered fabric. Backstitch a few stitches. Press seams away from center but do not trim.

5. Refer to Technique 9, Steps 4–5 on page 63. Rotate design assembly to the right so the first patchwork border is on the bottom. Select one

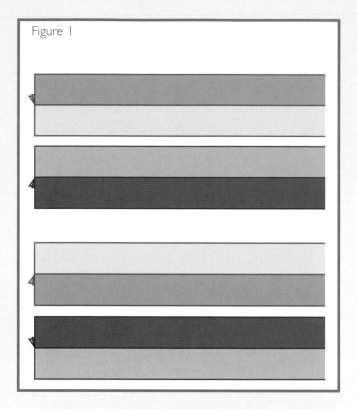

Figure 1

of the patchwork assemblies with the dark strips on the inside. With right sides together, pin the raw edge of the light red side to the right edge of embroidered fabric. Beginning at top edge again, sew together, taking ¼" seam allowance, stopping at raw edge of first patchwork border. Press seams away from center and trim second border even with edge of first border.

6. Rotate design assembly and repeat for the next side, using the remaining strip with dark strips on the outside.

7. To complete the final border, pin the remaining patchwork border to the design assembly. Beginning at the edge of the first border, sew together to raw edge of previous border, taking ¼" seam allowance. Press seams away from center and flip the first border to the top of the last border. (See Figure 2 on page 87) With right sides together, stitch the end of the first border to the last border, continuing stitching at

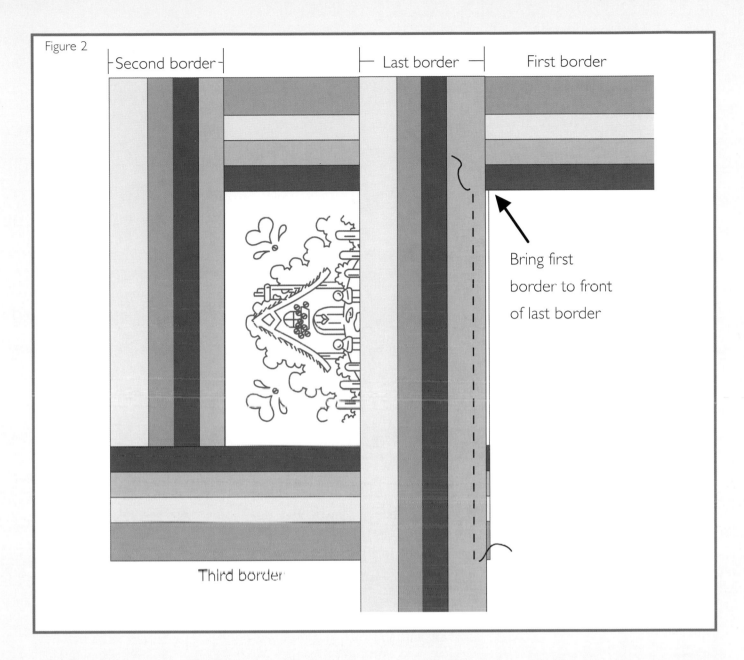

Figure 2

Second border

Last border

First border

Bring first
border to front
of last border

Third border

the point where the backstitching began. Trim edges and press.

Assemble the wall hanging

1. Cut a 3" x 7" strip from light tan fabric. Fold in half lengthwise, right sides together. Sew, taking a ½" seam allowance. Press seam open. Turn right sides out and press, centering seam.

2. Cut strip in half to make two 2" x 3½" pieces.

Fold one piece in half with seam allowance to the inside, then baste raw edges together. Repeat for remaining piece.

3. Lay patchwork top right side up on a hard flat surface, with raw edges matching. Pin tabs to top edge of patchwork and align tabs with the red strips on either side of the center design. Baste tabs in place.

4. Cut one 9½" square from light tan fabric for

Redwork Design

Do not transfer this outline onto fabric. Use it to align with grain of fabric.

Detail of Embroidery Stitches

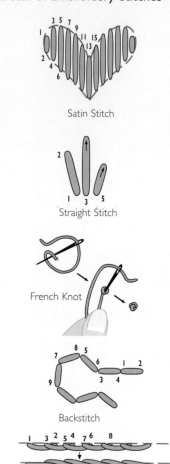

Satin Stitch

Straight Stitch

French Knot

Backstitch

Stem Stitch

Listing of Embroidery Stitches

Backstitch

interior lines of chimney, door, fence, leaves, flowers, stepping stones (1x)

other outlines (2x)

French Knot

● (2x)

◍ (3x)

Stem (2x)

"welcome", roof line, hill line

Straight (2x)

roof shingles

Satin (2x)

heart on door

backing. Cut one 9½" square from batting. Baste batting to wrong side of backing around the edges.

5. With right side of backing to right side of patchwork assembly, pin backing/batting to patchwork. Taking a ¼" seam allowance, sew around edges, leaving a 4" opening centered at the bottom.

6. Trim the corners and batting from seam allowances, turn right sides out, and press flat. Refer to Blind Stitch on page 26. Blind-stitch the opening closed.

7. Refer to Technique 3, Step 3 on page 40. Machine-quilt through all layers around center design, using the "Stitch in the Ditch" method.

8. Insert dowel through tabs and attach finial caps to ends of dowel.

How do I use sashing to combine traditional quilt block motifs?

Tradition and history are integral parts of quilt-making, and the Traditional Nine-block Sampler Quilt packs both into just 40 square inches. Each block is a well-known and loved traditional pattern. The setting (the arrangement of the blocks in the design) is another time-tested favorite: three rows of three blocks called the "Nine-patch."

Here's how:

Design Tips: Sashings (strips of fabric that separate the blocks) and borders are design elements common in historical quilts. In this one, (along with color) sashings serve to unify the different block patterns. The color choice is contemporary, but even that is traditional, as you look at how the colors of quilts have changed with the fashions of the day. Your color choices are the key to the look of this quilt. Be certain to consider the whole quilt as you choose, and not just the individual blocks.

Make the patchwork top

1. Make the nine different blocks shown in Figure 1 on page 90. *Note: All nine blocks use different combinations of the same 11 printed fabrics.*

2. After making the individual blocks, see page 107 for instructions on how to finish the quilt.

What you need to get started

Fabrics
44"—45"-wide 100% cotton

- ¼ yard each of 8–10 printed fabrics for patchwork top
- ⅝ yard antique dark red for borders and binding
- ⅞ yard medium antique red for sashing
- 1⅛ yards cream print for backing
- 1⅛ yards medium-weight quilt batting

Additional items
- ☑ Clear acetate or plastic for templates
- ☑ Freezer paper
- ☑ Iron
- ☑ Light-colored pencil
- ☑ Needles for hand sewing
- ☑ Permanent fine-point pen
- ☑ Quilter's ruler
- ☑ Rotary cutter
- ☑ Safety pins
- ☑ Sequin pins

- ☑ Sewing machine
- ☑ Sewing threads
- ☑ Small sharp scissors
- ☑ Straight pins
- ☑ Tan quilting thread
- ☑ Tweezers

Figure 1

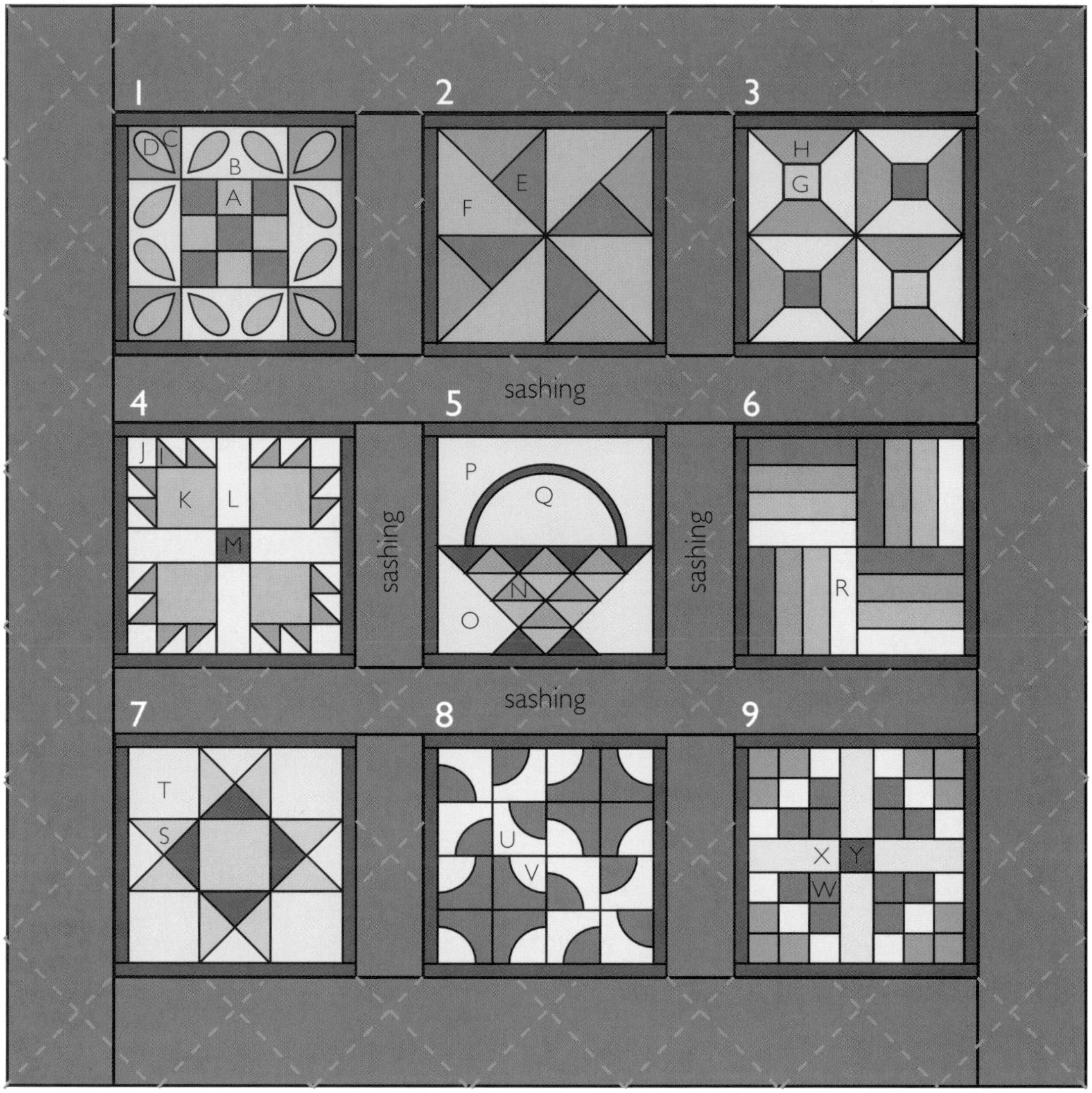

1
2
3
D
C
B
A
H
G
E
F
sashing
4
5
6
J
I
K
L
M
P
Q
sashing
sashing
N
O
R
sashing
7
8
9
T
S
U
V
X
Y
W

Fabric 1 - pale moss print

Fabric 2 - rose tan print

Fabric 3 - cream medium floral print

Fabric 4 - cream large floral print

Fabric 5 - cream small floral print

Fabric 6 - rose large floral print

Fabric 7 - gold red floral print

Fabric 8 - moss small floral print

Fabric 9 - red small floral print

Fabric 10 - deep burgundy print

Traditional Nine-block Sampler Quilt finished size: 40" square

1. Honey Bee Block, see page 92.
2. Pinwheel Block, see page 94.
3. Bow Tie Block, see page 96.
4. Bear Paw Block, see page 98.
5. Basket Block, see page 99.
6. Fence Rail Block, see page 102.
7. Ohio Star Block, see page 103.
8. Drunkard's Path Block, see page 105.
9. Nine-patch Hearts Block, see page 106.

Make the Honey Bee Block

1. Trace Honey Bee Template Patterns A, B, and C and cut out fabrics according to the cutting instructions on the patterns. Refer to Technique 5, Step 2, on page 48. Lay out fabrics as shown in Figure 3 on page 93.

2. Using an accurate ¼" seam allowance, sew the center column A pieces first, beginning with the middle of row 1. When all three rows are joined in the center, sew remaining A pieces in row 1 to row 2, then row 2 to row 3. Press seams in the direction indicated by arrows on Figure 3.

3. Assemble the remaining block pieces in sequence.

4. To make a smooth and accurate appliqué shape, cut out 12 pieces of template D from freezer paper. Place freezer paper pieces, shiny side down, on the wrong side of Fabric 5, leaving at least ½" around shapes. Refer to Technique 10, Steps 2–4, on page 67. Press paper pieces to fabric using a medium-hot dry iron on a hard flat surface.

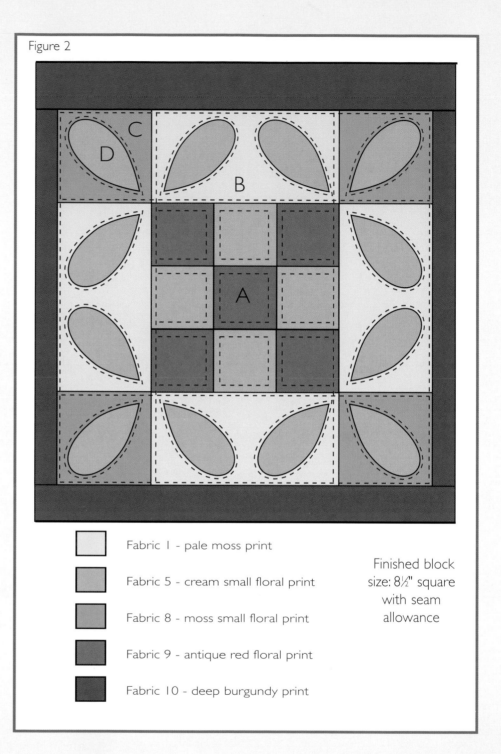

Figure 2

Fabric 1 - pale moss print

Fabric 5 - cream small floral print

Fabric 8 - moss small floral print

Fabric 9 - antique red floral print

Fabric 10 - deep burgundy print

Finished block size: 8½" square with seam allowance

5. Cut out fabric D pieces, adding ¼" seam allowance around edge of freezer paper.

6. Turn ¼" seam allowance snugly over edge of paper. Baste turned seam allowance in place through all layers with small running stitches. Begin and end basting thread at top for easy removal.

Honey Bee Template Patterns

Honey
Bee
A
Cut four - Fabric 5
Cut five - Fabric 9

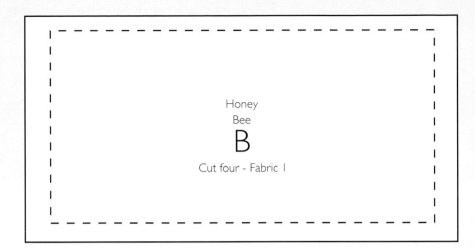

Honey
Bee
B
Cut four - Fabric 1

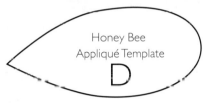

Honey Bee
Appliqué Template
D
Cut 12 - Freezer paper/Fabric 5

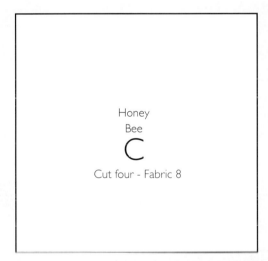

Honey
Bee
C
Cut four - Fabric 8

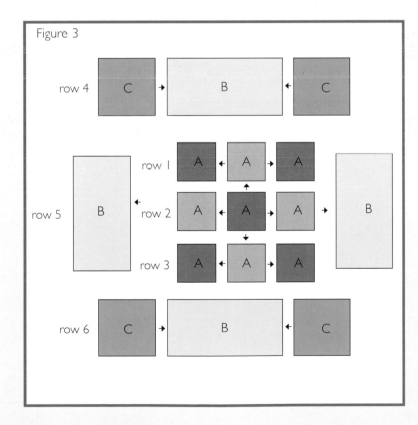

Figure 3

row 4   C → B ← C

row 1   A ← A → A

row 5   B ←   row 2   A ← A → A → B

row 3   A ← A → A

row 6   C → B ← C

7. Pin appliqué pieces in the positions indicated on Figure 2 on page 92. Refer to Blind Stitch on page 26. Using a blind stitch and matching thread, sew appliqué pieces to block. Remove basting stitches.

8. Turn block to wrong side and trim away fabric behind appliqué pieces, leaving ¼" seam allowances within the appliqué shapes. Remove freezer paper with tweezers.

9. Press completed block.

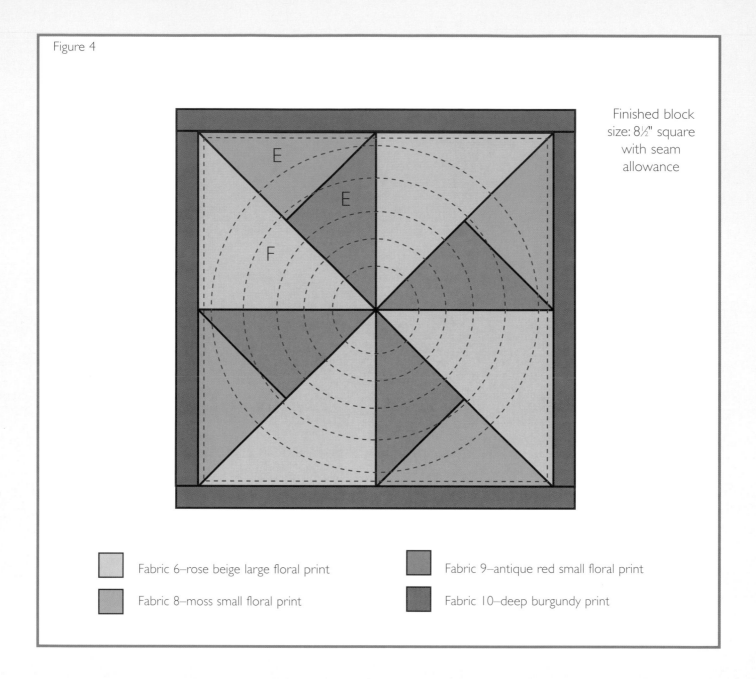

Figure 4

Finished block size: 8½" square with seam allowance

Fabric 6–rose beige large floral print

Fabric 8–moss small floral print

Fabric 9–antique red small floral print

Fabric 10–deep burgundy print

Make the Pinwheel Block

1. Trace Pinwheel Template Patterns E and F and cut out fabrics according to the cutting instructions on the patterns. Refer to Technique 5, Step 2, on page 48. Lay out cut fabrics as shown in Figure 5 on page 95.

2. Using an accurate ¼" seam allowance, sew two E pieces to one F piece. Repeat for three more blocks.

3. Rotate blocks into the positions shown in Figure 5 on page 95. Stitch top two blocks first, then bottom two, then sew row 1 to row 2. Press seams in the direction indicated by the arrows.

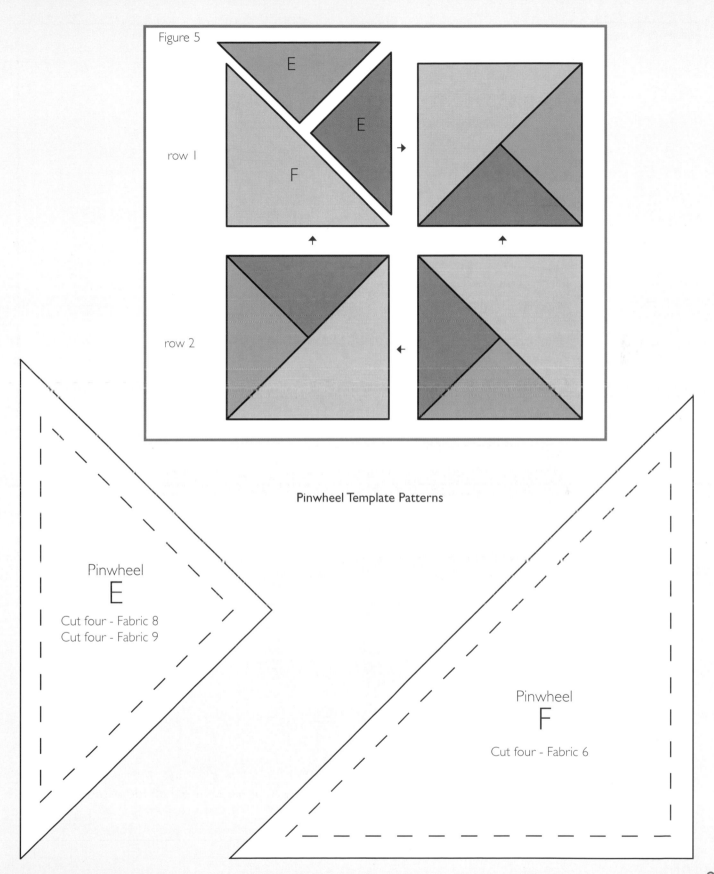

Figure 5

row 1

row 2

E

E

F

Pinwheel Template Patterns

Pinwheel
E

Cut four - Fabric 8
Cut four - Fabric 9

Pinwheel
F

Cut four - Fabric 6

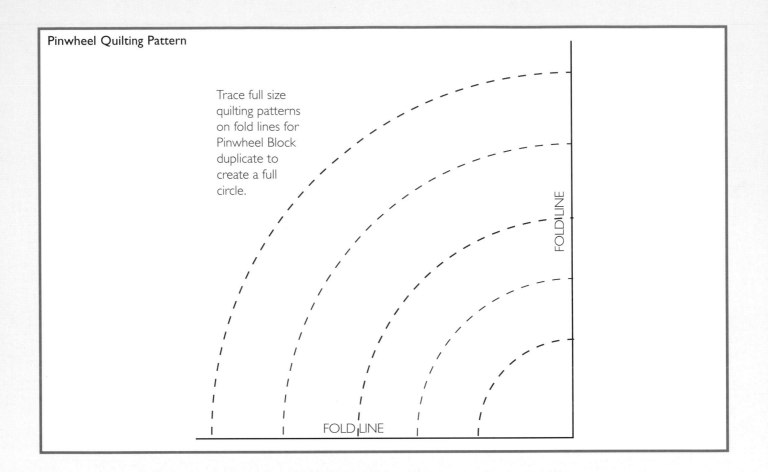

Pinwheel Quilting Pattern

Trace full size quilting patterns on fold lines for Pinwheel Block duplicate to create a full circle.

FOLDLINE

FOLD LINE

Make the Bow Tie Block

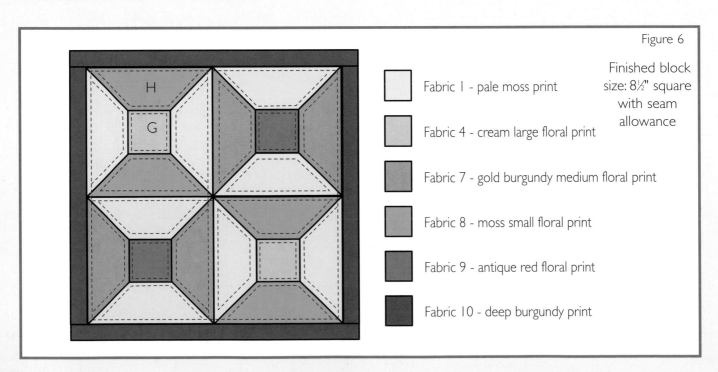

Figure 6

Finished block size: 8½" square with seam allowance

Fabric 1 - pale moss print

Fabric 4 - cream large floral print

Fabric 7 - gold burgundy medium floral print

Fabric 8 - moss small floral print

Fabric 9 - antique red floral print

Fabric 10 - deep burgundy print

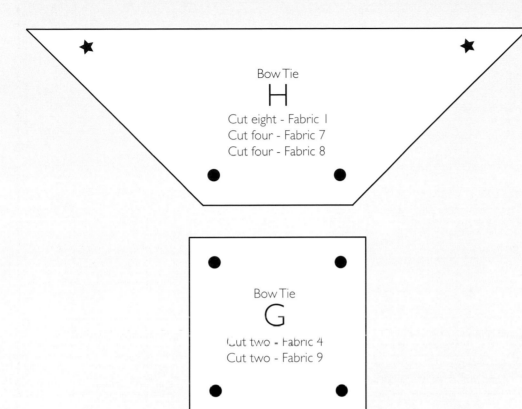

Bow Tie

H

Cut eight - Fabric 1
Cut four - Fabric 7
Cut four - Fabric 8

Bow Tie

G

Cut two - Fabric 4
Cut two - Fabric 9

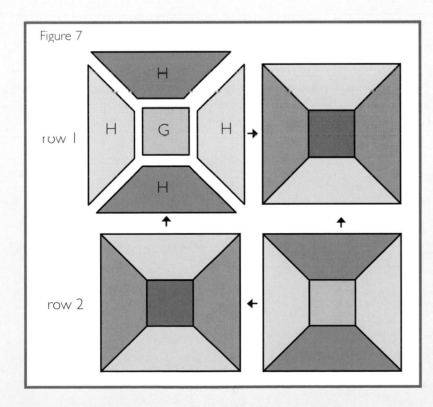

Figure 7

row 1

row 2

1. Trace Bow Tie Template Patterns G and H and cut out fabrics according to the instructions on the patterns. Refer to Technique 5, Step 2, on page 48. Lay out fabrics as shown in Figure 7.

2. Using a ¼" seam allowance, put the first block together by sewing a piece H to piece G, with right sides together, between dots, stopping and starting at dots. Rotate and sew remaining three H pieces to G in same manner.

3. Matching dots and stars on one side, sew on ¼" seam allowances from dot to star, right sides together. Repeat for remaining three sides. Trim seam allowance and press seams away from piece G and toward the darker colors on pieces H. Repeat for three more blocks.

4. Rotate blocks into position shown in Figure 7. Stitch top two blocks first, then bottom two, then sew row 1 to row 2. Press seams in the direction indicated by arrows.

Make the Bear Paw Block

Figure 8

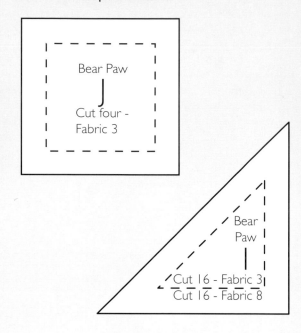

Fabric 3 - cream medium floral print

Fabric 6 - rose beige large floral print

Fabric 8 - moss small floral print

Fabric 10 - deep burgundy print

Finished block size: 8½" square with seam allowance

1. Trace Bear Paw Template Patterns I–M and cut out fabrics according to the cutting instructions on the patterns. Refer to Technique 5, Step 2, on page 48.

Bear Paw
J
Cut four - Fabric 3

Bear Paw
I
Cut 16 - Fabric 3
Cut 16 - Fabric 8

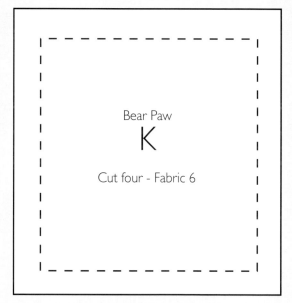

Bear Paw
K
Cut four - Fabric 6

Bear Paw
M
Cut one - Fabric 10

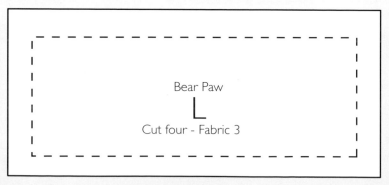

Bear Paw
L
Cut four - Fabric 3

2. Sew the two colors of triangles together to make 16 small squares, using an accurate ¼" seam allowance. Press seams toward the darker color.

3. Referring to Figure 9, construct the four "paw" blocks. Press seams in direction of arrows.

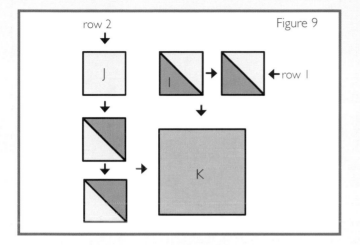

Figure 9

Make the Basket Block

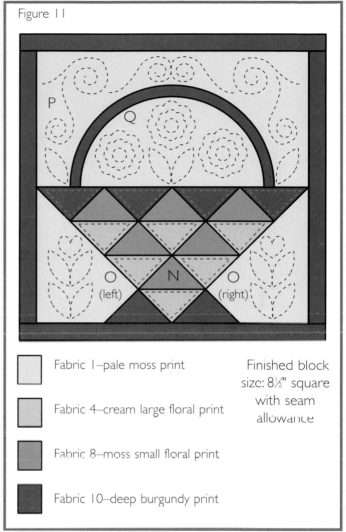

Figure 11

Fabric 1—pale moss print

Fabric 4—cream large floral print

Fabric 8—moss small floral print

Fabric 10—deep burgundy print

Finished block size: 8½" square with seam allowance

4. Lay out paw blocks and remaining fabrics as shown in Figure 10 and join pieces into rows, using an accurate ¼" seam allowance. Matching seams, sew row 1 to row 2 and row 2 to row 3. Press seams in the direction indicated by arrows.

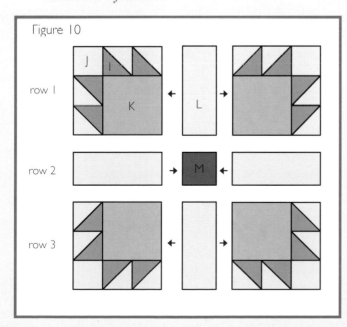

Figure 10

1. Trace Basket Template Patterns N, O, and Q on page 100. Cut out fabrics according to the cutting instructions on the patterns. Refer to Technique 5, Step 2, on page 48. For piece O, cut one piece for the right side of the basket with pattern right side up, and one piece for the left side with the pattern right side down. Cut pattern piece P on page 101 on fold line (See Figure 11)

2. Referring to Figure 12 on page 101, construct the basket, using a ¼" seam allowance. Sew all the N pieces of fabric 4 and fabric 8 together

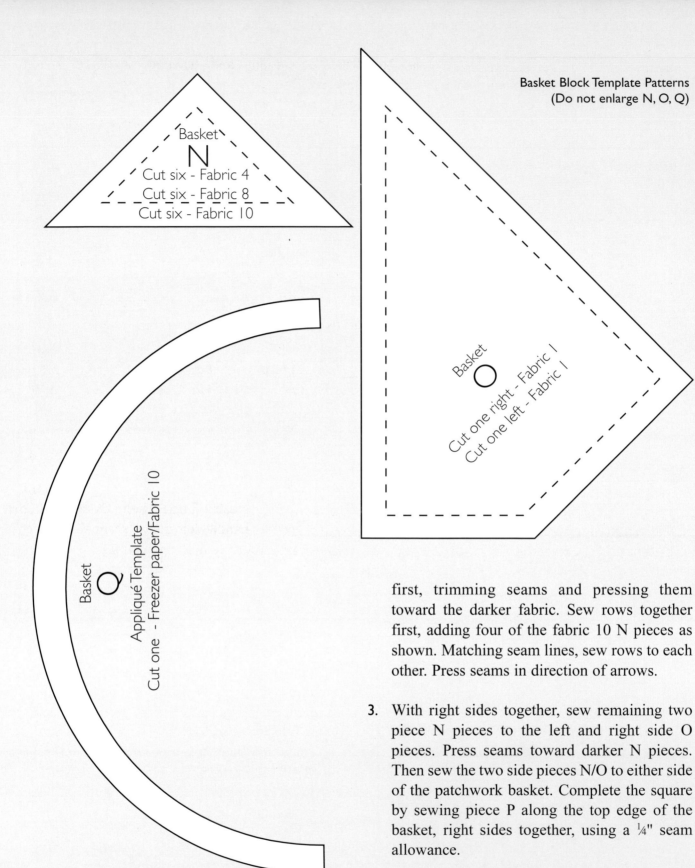

Basket

N

Cut six - Fabric 4

Cut six - Fabric 8

Cut six - Fabric 10

Basket

O

Cut one right - Fabric 1

Cut one left - Fabric 1

Basket

Q

Appliqué Template

Cut one - Freezer paper/Fabric 10

first, trimming seams and pressing them toward the darker fabric. Sew rows together first, adding four of the fabric 10 N pieces as shown. Matching seam lines, sew rows to each other. Press seams in direction of arrows.

3. With right sides together, sew remaining two piece N pieces to the left and right side O pieces. Press seams toward darker N pieces. Then sew the two side pieces N/O to either side of the patchwork basket. Complete the square by sewing piece P along the top edge of the basket, right sides together, using a ¼" seam allowance.

Basket
P
Cut one on fold - Fabric 1

FOLD LINE

4. To make a smooth and accurate appliqué shape, trace template Q onto freezer paper and cut out. Place paper piece, plastic side down, on the wrong side of fabric 10, leaving at least ¼" around all sides. Press paper pieces onto fabric, using a medium-hot dry iron on a hard flat surface.

5. Refer to Technique 10, Steps 3–4 on page 67. Cut out fabric Q piece, adding ¼" seam allowance around edge of freezer paper.

6. Turn ¼" seam allowance snugly over edge of paper. Baste turned seam allowance in place through all layers with small running stitches. Begin and end basting thread on top for easy removal.

7. Pin appliqué handle in position indicated on Figure 11 on page 99. Refer to Blind Stitch on page 26. Using a blind-stitch and matching thread, sew appliqué pieces to block. Remove basting stitches.

8. Turn block to wrong side and slash fabric behind appliquéd handle, leaving ¼" seam allowances within the appliqué shape. Remove freezer paper with tweezers.

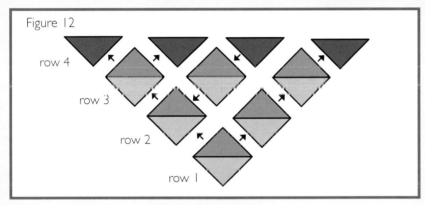

Figure 12

row 4

row 3

row 2

row 1

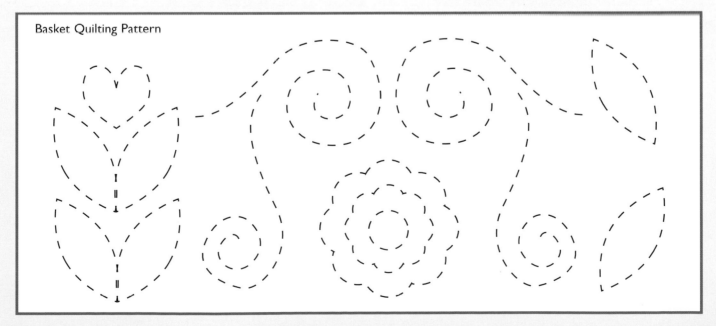

Basket Quilting Pattern

Make the Fence Rail Block

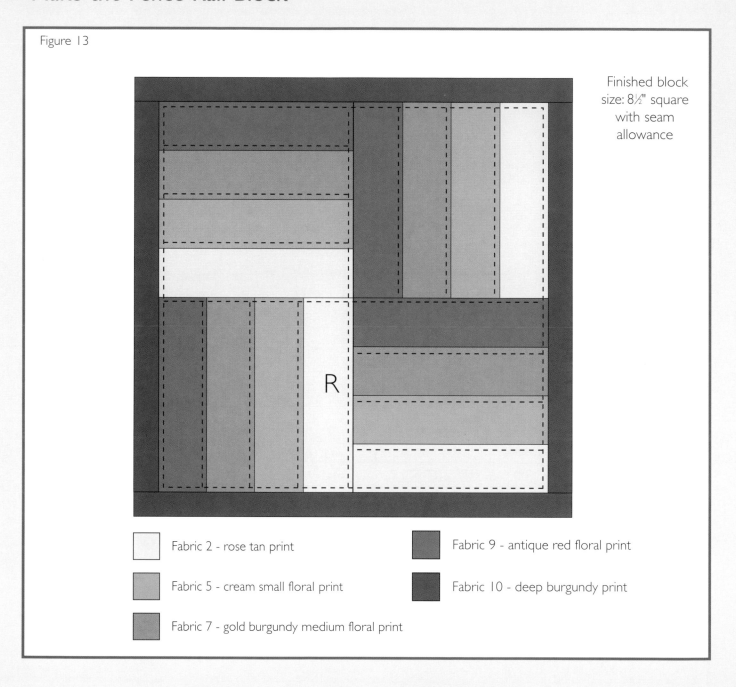

Figure 13

Finished block size: 8½" square with seam allowance

R

Fabric 2 - rose tan print

Fabric 5 - cream small floral print

Fabric 7 - gold burgundy medium floral print

Fabric 9 - antique red floral print

Fabric 10 - deep burgundy print

1. Cut one 1½" x 18" strip from each of the four fabrics listed.
   - Fabric 2
   - Fabric 7
   - Fabric 5
   - Fabric 9

2. Cut 1½" x 4½" for piece R from freezer paper.

3. With right sides together, sew strips together, using a ¼" seam allowance (See Piecing in Glossary on page 110). Press seams toward darker fabrics. Use piece R as a guide, and cut pieced fabric strips into four equal pieces. See Figure 14 on page 103.

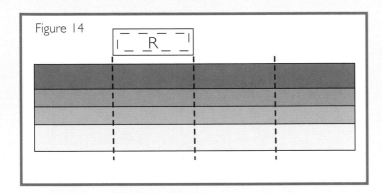

Figure 14

Make the Ohio Star Block

1. Trace Ohio Star Template Patterns S and T onto three fabrics. Cut out fabrics according to the cutting instructions on the templates.

2. Using an accurate ¼" seam allowance and matching stars, sew four S pieces together, using the three different colors. (See Figure 16) Trim points and press seams in direction indicated by the arrows. Repeat for four squares.

3. Rotate S blocks and lay out with remaining T pieces as shown in Figure 17 on page 104. Stitch rows together in order. Sew row 1 to row 2.

4. Rotate cut pieces into the positions shown in Figure 15. With right sides together and using a ¼" seam allowance, sew top two blocks together into row 1.

5. Repeat for bottom two blocks for row 2. Sew the two rows together to complete the block. Press seams in direction of arrows.

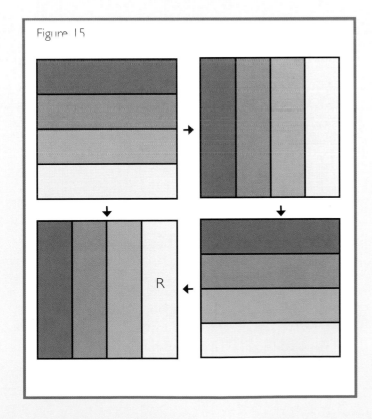

Figure 15

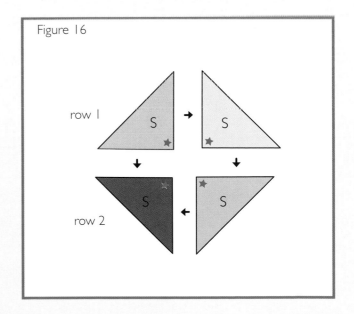

Figure 16

Ohio Star Template Patterns

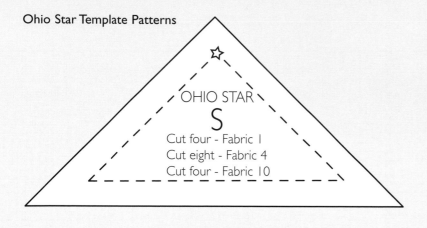

OHIO STAR
S
Cut four - Fabric 1
Cut eight - Fabric 4
Cut four - Fabric 10

Finished block
size: 8½" square
with seam
allowance

Ohio Star Quilting Pattern

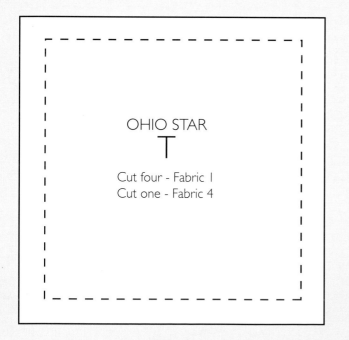

OHIO STAR
T

Cut four - Fabric 1
Cut one - Fabric 4

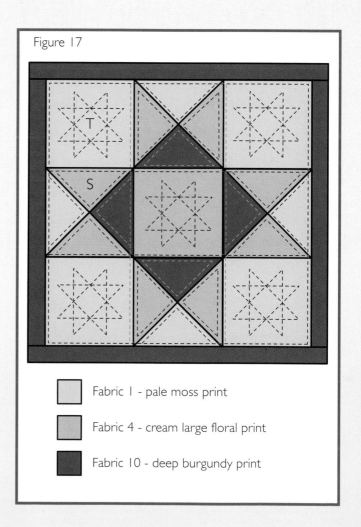

Figure 17

Fabric 1 - pale moss print

Fabric 4 - cream large floral print

Fabric 10 - deep burgundy print

Make the Drunkard's Path Block

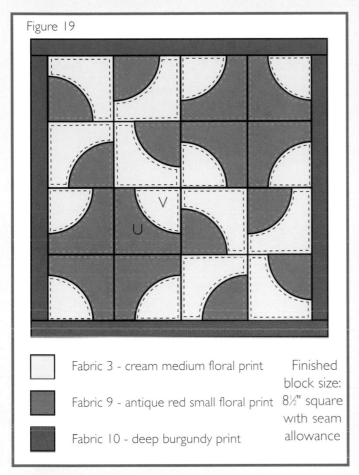

Figure 19

	Fabric 3 - cream medium floral print
	Fabric 9 - antique red small floral print
	Fabric 10 - deep burgundy print

Finished block size: 8½" square with seam allowance

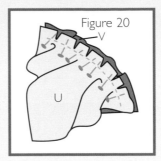

Figure 20

with dark U pieces sewn to light V pieces and eight with fabrics reversed.

4. Referring to Figure 21, rotate squares into position and sew, right sides together, in rows, using an accurate ¼" seam allowance. Press seams in direction of arrows. Complete block by sewing rows together. (See Figure 19) Press seams downward.

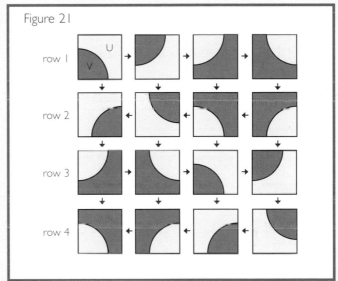

Figure 21

row 1
row 2
row 3
row 4

1. Trace template patterns U and V and cut out fabrics according to the cutting instructions on the patterns.

2. With right sides together and matching dots and raw curved edges, pin one U piece to a V piece of the opposite color, clipping and easing U piece to fit the curve of V piece. (See Figure 20) Sew over pins or basting on an accurate ¼" seam allowance. Remove pins or basting thread.

3. Assemble 16 U/V squares from remaining pieces; eight

Drunkard's Path Template Patterns

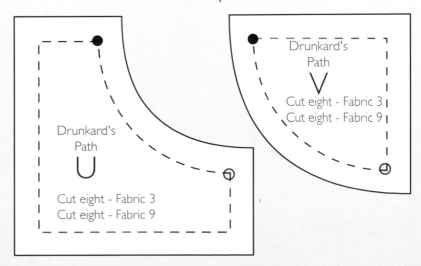

Drunkard's Path U
Cut eight - Fabric 3
Cut eight - Fabric 9

Drunkard's Path V
Cut eight - Fabric 3
Cut eight - Fabric 9

Make the Nine-patch Hearts Block

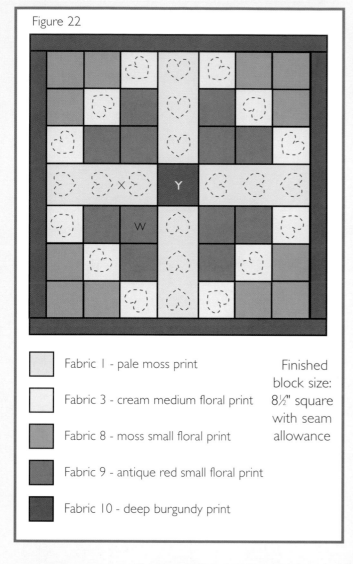

Figure 22

Fabric 1 - pale moss print

Fabric 3 - cream medium floral print

Fabric 8 - moss small floral print

Fabric 9 - antique red small floral print

Fabric 10 - deep burgundy print

Finished block size: 8½" square with seam allowance

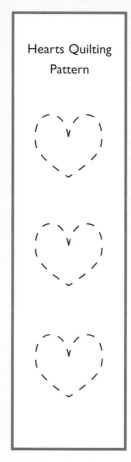

Hearts Quilting Pattern

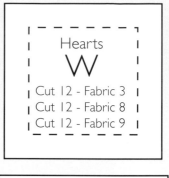

Hearts
W
Cut 12 - Fabric 3
Cut 12 - Fabric 8
Cut 12 - Fabric 9

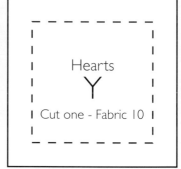

Hearts
Y
Cut one - Fabric 10

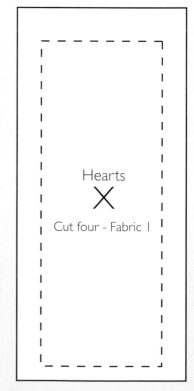

Hearts
X
Cut four - Fabric 1

1. From each of the three fabrics listed on pattern W, cut one 1⅝" x 20" strip of fabric. Trace pattern W onto freezer paper and cut out. Use as template to cut 12 W pieces from each strip. Trace template patterns X and Y and cut out fabrics according to the cutting instructions on the patterns.

2. Assemble each nine-patch block following Figure 23 on page 107. Using an accurate ¼" seam allowance, sew W pieces, right sides together, in rows. Press seams in directions of arrows. Complete the block by sewing rows together. Repeat for three more blocks with remaining W pieces.

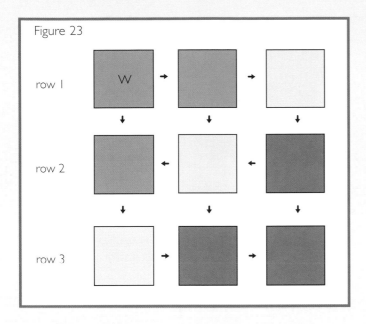

Figure 23

row 1

row 2

row 3

3. Referring to Figure 24, lay out completed blocks with piece X and Y fabrics. Sew rows first, pressing seams in direction of arrows. Complete the block by sewing rows together. See Figure 22 on page 106.

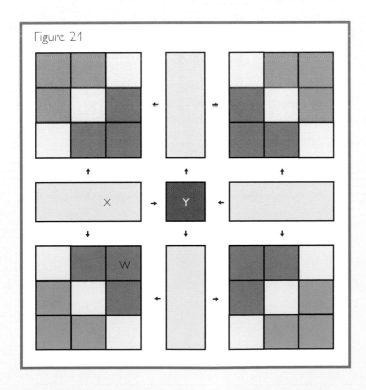

Figure 24

Finish the quilt

Add block borders

1. Using fabric 10, cut nine strips 1" wide by the width of the fabric. Trim off selvage edges. All unbordered blocks should measure 8½" square. The finished blocks with borders will be 9½" square.

2. Use the stitch-and-trim method to add borders to all nine blocks as follows: Beginning at a corner, pin a strip to top edge of first block, right sides together and matching raw edges. Refer to Setting Elements on pages 17–18. Sew, using ¼" seam allowance. Trim strip off at the corner and press seams toward the strip.

3. Using the same fabric 10 strip and the same method, add a border to the bottom edge; trim and press. Add side borders, overlapping top and bottom borders. Press seams toward strips and square block.

Add sashing

1. Using fabric 9, cut four strips 3" wide by the width of the fabric. Trim off selvage edges. From two of these strips, cut six 9½" lengths.

2. Arrange blocks and sashing strips as shown in Figure 25 on page 108, with 9½" sashing between blocks. Refer to Setting Elements on pages 17–18. Using an accurate ¼" seam allowance, sew blocks and sashing together into three rows. Then sew rows to long sashing strips. Trim excess sashing and press seams in direction of arrows.

3. Using fabric 9, cut four strips 4½" wide by the width of the fabric. Trim off selvage edges.

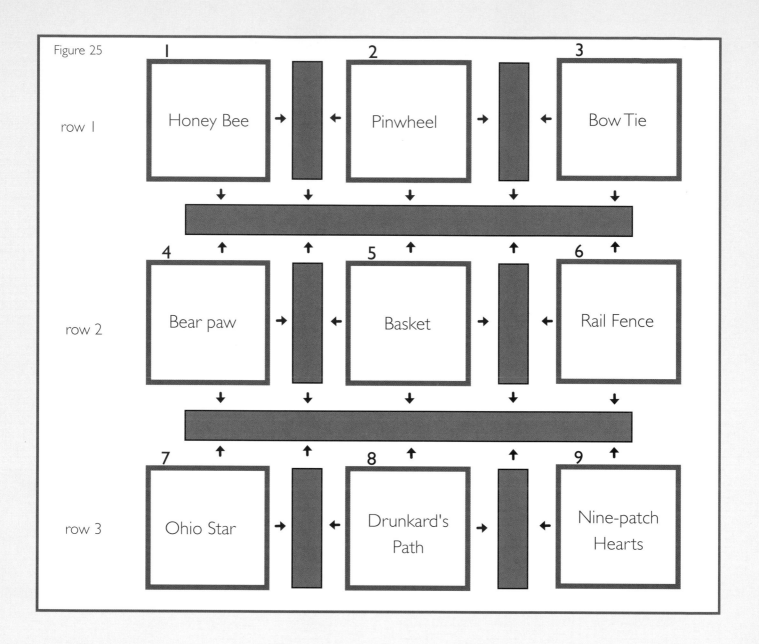

Figure 25

row 1 — 1 Honey Bee — 2 Pinwheel — 3 Bow Tie

row 2 — 4 Bear paw — 5 Basket — 6 Rail Fence

row 3 — 7 Ohio Star — 8 Drunkard's Path — 9 Nine-patch Hearts

4. Refer to Technique 9, Steps 2–5 on pages 62–63. Using the stitch-and-trim method and a ¼" seam allowance, add borders to assembled quilt as for block borders. Refer to How do I bind a quilt? on pages 26–27. Sew top and bottom strips first, then sides. Trim excess border strips and press seams toward borders.

Assemble the sampler

1. Cut a 40" square of backing fabric and a 40" square of batting. Press the patchwork top and backing fabric.

2. Referring to Figure 1 on page 90, mark the diagonal quilting lines on the quilt border so that there is 8" between the points. Referring to the quilt lines marked on the individual block diagrams, transfer the full-sized quilt patterns to the following blocks:

- Pinwheel, page 94, Figure 4
- Basket, page 99, Figure 11

- Ohio Star, page 104, Figure 17
- Nine-patch Hearts, page 106, Figure 22

3. Lay the backing fabric on a flat clean surface, right side down. Refer to How do I assemble a quilt? on pages 23–24. Center the quilt batting on top of the backing fabric and the patchwork top, right side up, on the batting. Smooth out any folds in the layers as you go. Batting/backing will extend beyond all sides of quilt top.

4. Starting in the center of the quilt, baste or safety-pin the layers together. Work from the center out in rows about 4" apart.

Quilt the sampler

1. Refer to How do I quilt the layers together? on page 24–26. Using a quilt stitch and quilting thread in a quilt hoop, begin quilting the center basket block. Quilt on transferred design lines in the solid areas. Referring to Figure 11 on page 99, quilt interior "Basket" pieces $\frac{1}{16}$" from seam lines. Remove any basting stitches.

2. Quilt remaining blocks as for Basket, working outward from center and referring to individual block diagrams for quilt patterns. Referring to Figure 1 on page 90, quilt the borders when all blocks have been quilted.

3. Baste layers together just inside the edge of patchwork top. Trim batting and backing to $\frac{1}{4}$" beyond patchwork top to create a $\frac{1}{2}$" seam allowance around edges.

Bind the quilt

1. Cut four 3" x 44" strips from fabric 10.

2. Make a mitered corner binding. Refer to Technique 3, Steps 7–9 on pages 40–41. Refer to How do I bind a quilt on page 26. Press strips in half lengthwise, wrong sides together, then press one long edge under $\frac{1}{4}$" on each binding strip. Fold lengths in half and mark centers.

3. With a pencil, mark a dot $\frac{1}{4}$" in from each corner of the quilt top.

4. Right sides together, center and pin one 44" binding strip on the left edge of quilt top, matching unfolded raw edge of strip to raw edge of border. Binding should extend approximately $2\frac{1}{2}$" beyond top edge of sampler. Sew strip to sampler along $\frac{1}{4}$" seam allowance, stopping at the marked dot. Backstitch several stitches from the dot. Repeat with another strip on opposite side.

5. Transfer dot marking to binding. Fold and press binding ends at a 45° angle from marked dot, pin out of the way.

6. Center and pin top and bottom bindings, as for side bindings, stopping at marked dots. Fold and press binding ends at a 45° angle as for the sides.

7. Pin overlapping bindings together matching center fold lines, raw edges and pressed edges. On top binding, draw a line from end of seam (marked dot) to the folded edges of bindings (a). From this line, measure along center fold line of binding $\frac{1}{2}$" (finished binding width), and mark (b) with a dot. Draw lines connecting points (a) to (b) and (b) to the original dot (c).

8. Holding binding together at (a), pull binding away from patchwork, and stitch from (a) to (b) to (c), flattening the point at (b) slightly (See page 41, Figure 4). Repeat for remaining three corners. Trim ends $\frac{1}{4}$" from seams.

9. Flip binding to back, press, pin, and blind-stitch to back.

10. Wrap and store your quilt.

Glossary

Appliqué. Attaching small shapes of fabric to a background fabric, either by hand or machine.

Basting. Securing all layers of a quilt so that they will not shift when quilted. This can be done with safety pins, stitches, or a basting gun.

Baste-stitch. A running stitch used to temporarily secure a piece before stitching.

Batting. The layer between the quilt top and the backing consisting of cotton, polyester, or a blend that gives extra warmth and body to quilts.

Betweens. Short, strong needles used for quilting by hand. Also used for hand-piecing.

Bias. Stretchy diagonal grain of fabric. A true bias is at a 45° angle to the straight grain.

Bindings. Strips of fabric used to finish off the edges of a quilt or quilt block.

Blind-stitch. Also called appliqué stitch. A small stitch worked inside the fold of the seam allowance when the stitching should not show.

Block. One unit of a quilt top. May also be used alone to make a smaller project. A block might be pieced, appliquéd, or a combination of them.

Borders. Edges added to the blocks or top and sides of the completed quilt top.

Corners. Sewing the corners of the borders at a 45° angle.

Crazy piecing. Sewing a variety of irregular shapes to a foundation fabric. The seams are then often embellished with embroidery stitches and other items such as beads, buttons, and ribbons.

Crewel needle. A sharp thin needle with a long eye used for laying fine threads on the surface of fabric.

Cross grain. The weft of the fabric that runs the width of the fabric.

Embroidery stitches. Embellishing stitches used to enhance or decorate. They are used extensively in crazy quilting.

Foundation. Material used as a base on which to sew smaller pieces of fabric. This can be temporary or permanent.

Framer's points. Small metal pieces can be used to attach artwork into frames.

Freezer paper. Heavy white paper with a plastic coating on one side that can be found in grocery stores. Used for template patterns.

Hand-quilting. Short straight running stitches done with quilting thread and a between needle to secure the layers of the quilt together.

Lengthwise grain. Threads of the fabric that are the warp and run parallel to the selvage.

Machine quilting. Using the sewing machine to quilt the layers together rather than by hand. Machine quilting is stronger than hand-quilting.

Marking tools. Pencils, pens, or chalks used to make the quilting patterns for quilting.

Mirror image. An image that is the exact opposite for the original.

Outline quilting. Quilting around a motif, usually an appliqué, approximately ⅛" from the edge to enhance the motif. Also called "echo" quilting.

Piecing. Using small portions of fabric to build a larger pattern, somewhat like a puzzle.

Posts. The squares of fabric used to join the ends of the sashing to quilt blocks.

Pressing seams. Using an iron to press the seams in one direction or another to reduce bulk in the seams and strengthen the seams.

Quilter's knot. A knot used in hand-quilting that is small and will slip through one layer of the fabric into the center of the sandwich.

Quilter's ruler. Clear rulers used by quilters with angles, inch, and metric measurements that can be placed directly on the fabric to make straight cuts.

Quilting patterns. Lines of stitching made by using stencils, or a freehand design to enhance the final look of the quilt. These patterns can be done by hand or machine.

Quilt sandwich. The three layers together consisting of the quilt top, batting and backing.

Quilting stencils. A piece of Mylar® with narrow slits cut in a design that allow a marking tool to contact the fabric below to trace the design.

Rotary cutter. A fabric cutting tool that consists of a circular cutting edge blade on a handle that is capable of cutting through layers of fabric. Used with a cutting mat.

Rotary cutting mat. A special mat designed to be used with a rotary cutter.

Rotary cutting ruler. A thick clear, acrylic ruler made for use with a rotary cutter.

Sashing. The strips of fabric sewn between quilt blocks to create a lattice effect.

Scissors. Sharp shears for fabric, craft scissors for paper or Mylar.

Seam allowance. Usually ¼" for quilting; this is the distance between the edge of the fabric and the seam line.

Selvage. Tightly woven edge that runs the length of both sides of the fabric.

Strip-piecing. A technique where long strips of fabric are cut to specific widths and lengths and sewn together lengthwise. Segments are then cut from these strips and sewn together in a new combination.

Template. A reusable copy of the pattern used as a guide for cutting out the pieces. May be cut from Mylar.

Tracing paper. See-through paper used to copy patterns and pattern layouts to transfer to the quilt blocks.

Zigzag stitch. A machine stitch used to secure appliqués to quilted items, adding style and strength.

Metric eqivalency chart

inches to centimeters

inches	cm	inches	cm
⅛	0.3	5	12.7
¼	0.6	6	15.2
⅜	1.0	7	17.8
½	1.3	8	20.3
⅝	1.6	9	22.9
¾	1.9	10	25.4
⅞	2.2	11	27.9
1	2.5	12	30.5
1¼	3.2	13	33.0
1½	3.8	14	35.6
1¾	4.4	15	38.1
2	5.1	16	40.6
2½	6.4	20	50.8
3	7.6	30	76.2
3½	8.9	40	101.6
4	10.2	44	111.8
4½	11.4	45	114.3

yards to metres

yards	metres	yards	metres
⅛	0.11	2	1.83
¼	0.23	2 ⅛	1.94
⅜	0.34	2 ¼	2.06
½	0.46	2 ⅜	2.17
⅝	0.57	2 ½	2.29
¾	0.69	2 ⅝	2.40
⅞	0.80	2 ¾	2.51
1	0.91	2 ⅞	2.63
1⅛	1.03	3	2.74
1¼	1.14	4	3.66
1⅜	1.26	5	4.57
1½	1.37	6	5.49
1⅝	1.49	7	6.40
1¾	1.60	8	7.32
1⅞	1.71	9	8.23
		10	9.14

Index

About Kooler Design Studio

Since the establishment of Kooler Design Studio, in 1985, it has been my pleasure to work with an exceptionally creative group of designers, editors, photographers, and writers. Our goal has always been to provide great design and beautiful images, accompanied with easy-to-read and accurate instructions, all provided to inspire and nourish your creative soul.

Quilting is one of my favorite pastimes because it uses all the elements I love, fiber, fabric, color, and design. Writer/editor JoLynn Taylor, along with designers Nancy Wong and Sandy Orton have done a superb job of producing my collection of projects for the first-time quilter. You will find easy-to-follow step-by-step directions, drawings, and beautiful photographs. Within hours, you'll be creating keepsakes for friends and family.

Donna Kooler